Clinical Social Work with Maltreated Children and Their Families

Clinical Social Work with Maltreated Children and Their Families

An Introduction to Practice

Edited by
Shirley M. Ehrenkranz
Eda G. Goldstein
Lawrence Goodman
Jeffrey Seinfeld

New York University Press
New York and London

Library of Congress Cataloging-in-Publication Data

Clinical social work with maltreated children and their families : an
introduction to practice / edited by Shirley M. Ehrenkranz . . . [et
al.].
p.   cm.
Includes bibliographies and index.
ISBN 0-8147-2174-5 (alk. paper)   ISBN 0-8147-2175-3
(pbk. : alk. paper)
1. Family social work—United States.   2. Social work with
children—United States   3. Abused children—Services for—United
States.   4. Family psychotherapy—United States.   I. Ehrenkranz,
Shirley M., 1920–
HV699.C53   1989
362.7'044—dc19   88-28987
                                                          CIP

Contents

v

Acknowledgments

To Marianne Gerschel, whose deep concern for the welfare of children and generous support of the New York University School of Social Work made this book possible.

To the writers, for their insights and their dedication in preparing a book that attempts to enhance the knowledge and skills of the social work practitioner.

To social work practitioners, who day-in and day-out make the difference in so many lives.

To the children and their families, who are our future.

Introduction

Shirley M. Ehrenkranz, D.S.W.

Most writing on maltreated children and their families has been polemical, policy oriented, or historical. Little has been available that speaks directly to the social work practitioner as she or he confronts the complex problems of working with this population. We wrote this book for other practitioners and students as practitioners ourselves. Mindful of the fact that child protective services are provided by individuals with different levels of practice knowledge, the book was planned for beginning workers as well as those with specialized training.

The New York University School of Social Work's graduate programs focus on clinical social work. The faculty includes many scholars who have specialized knowledge and skill in working with children and their families, and the school regularly conducts workshops and symposia for practitioners in this field. Our training and demonstration projects in child welfare have received extensive support from the United States Office of Human Development Services, Administration for Children, Youth, and Families, as well as from many other sources, public and private.

This book reflects the school's approach in teaching direct practice. The curriculum provides students with a holistic view of social work practice rather than one narrowly tied to method. It teaches an integrative approach that enables students to work across different systems—individual, family, small group, organization, neighborhood, and community. Students learn to make broad-gauged assessments,

I

to apply a variety of modalities, and to assume a range of social work roles in order to respond effectively to the needs of their clients. The contributors have each brought their own specialized knowledge and points of view, but they have also worked collaboratively with the editors to produce a unified work.

The range and complexity of the factors related to child abuse require a careful selection of areas of emphasis in a book of this scope. There is so much that is not yet tested or even understood, for example, about causal factors or effective methods of intervention. Nevertheless, the book represents a beginning. It is hoped that it will be a catalyst for subsequent publications specifically designed to help the social work practitioner deal with one of society's most critical areas of concern.

1

Child Maltreatment: An Overview

Gladys Gonzalez-Ramos, D.S.W., and
Eda G. Goldstein, D.S.W.

Introduction

Child maltreatment is on the rise. Yearly estimates of the number of abused and neglected children vary from one-half million to as many as four million. While cruelty to children has a long history, our society has avoided dealing with it as a social problem until recently. The neglect of maltreatment has been fostered by religious and societal values stressing stern discipline and corporal punishment, an emphasis on individual privacy, and a view that children are the property of their parents.

The social work profession pioneered efforts to confront and ameliorate this tragic social problem. When social work evolved in the late nineteenth and early twentieth centuries, many of its early leaders attempted to raise society's consciousness about child maltreatment and to pressure for social legislation that would protect children and their rights, particularly with respect to child labor. Social work practitioners were on the front lines in dealing with abused and neglected children and their families. Societal interest in child abuse and neglect fluctuated, however, until 1962, when Dr. Henry Kempe first coined the phrase *the battered child*. Kempe's work ushered in a new era in the awareness and study of child maltreatment.

3

The past twenty-five years have witnessed a new concern and growing anguish over the plight of maltreated children. In 1974 the United States Congress passed the Child Abuse Prevention and Treatment Act. It stipulated that in order for states to qualify for financial assistance they needed to enact a state child abuse-and-neglect law that would provide for reporting of known and suspected instances of maltreatment, immunity for those reporting, a mechanism for prompt investigation, and assurance of a state wide service system. With further impetus from Title XX amendments to the Social Security Act, all fifty states had enacted such legislation by 1978. Programs aimed at child maltreatment are extensive. They represent an important beginning in the prevention and treatment of child abuse and neglect.

The challenge to find and implement successful approaches to work with this difficult population still lies ahead of us. Although there is very little research on the outcome of treatment of abuse and neglect cases, the findings that are available are disappointing. It is not clear what models of clinical practice work with particular types of child maltreatment cases. Often practice approaches are dictated by the specific philosophy, bias, or expertise of the agency or practitioner rather than by systematic criteria. Collaboration among those involved in child maltreatment cases and coordination of services are fragmented. Amelioration of the social conditions, attitudes, and policies that contribute to child abuse and neglect has been stalled by other national priorities. Practitioners who struggle with these difficult and disturbing cases receive little support. They feel alone and become overwhelmed and often "burned out." There are no simple solutions to this grim state of affairs, but our clinical knowledge and experience do point to many positive directions. While work with maltreatment cases requires individualization, empathy, creativity, and flexibility, practitioners can benefit from a clinical practice perspective that provides them with a framework for understanding and addressing the multifaceted needs of this population.

What Is Child Maltreatment?

Kempe et al. (1962) originally used the term *battered child* to describe children who were seriously injured physically, but child

maltreatment encompasses more than physical abuse. The large majority of children who are reported to child protective services show
limited physical harm or none at all. These neglect cases, although
difficult to pinpoint, are far more prevalent and can have equally
devastating effects (McCabe 1986). Further, the growing incidence of
cases of sexual abuse confronts practitioners with new and vexing
clinical problems.

There are differing definitions of *child maltreatment* in the literature and in the legislation of various states. In order to maintain
consistency in terminology, this book will adhere to the most frequent
usage, viewing *maltreatment* as a descriptive and inclusive term for
all physical abuse or marked neglect of children. Accordingly, an
abused child is one whose parents or caretakers inflict or permit injury
or protracted impairment of physical or emotional health or allow
the risk of such injury. A *neglected child* is one whose physical,
mental, or emotional condition has been impaired or is in imminent
danger of becoming impaired as a result of the parents' or caretakers'
failing to supply adequate basic care, supervision, or guardianship; or
a child who has been abandoned by the person legally responsible for
his or her care. Sexual abuse is one form of child abuse that involves
the committing of sexual offenses or the allowing of such offenses to
be committed. This book will focus on both physical abuse and
neglect and will not deal specifically with the important and growing
problem of sexual abuse, the dynamics and treatment of which appear
to differ significantly from other types of physical abuse and neglect
(Frude 1981; Gil 1970).

Who Is Affected by Child Maltreatment?

Our understanding of the extent of child maltreatment and of
the social characteristics of abused and neglected children is based on
the number of confirmed cases. Thus statistics on maltreatment represent a smaller number of cases than those that are reported, and
they do not include unreported cases. Since reporting rates are influenced by social class and race, among other factors, the data may
overrepresent low-income and minority children (Hampton and Newberger 1985; O'Toole, Turbett, and Nalepka 1983).

According to the most comprehensive attempt to measure the frequency of child maltreatment, a study conducted by the American Association for Protecting Children, a division of the American Humane Association, more than 1.5 million children were reported to child protective services in 1983. Nearly 50 percent of the cases were opened after initial investigations. Of these opened cases, only 63 percent received service, perhaps suggesting an overemphasis on reporting and an underemphasis on service (Newberger 1983).

The data showed that neglect cases were far more frequent than abuse cases and that the greatest amount of serious physical abuse and neglect was committed against children under five years of age. The average age for all the cases of child maltreatment was 7.1 years and the cases were about equally divided between male and female. The findings also point to a strong relationship between minority status, social deprivation, single parenting, female-headed households, and child maltreatment.

What Are the Causes of Child Maltreatment?

There is no single explanation for child maltreatment. A complex interaction of biological, psychological, environmental, and societal factors occurs in most cases. The crucial determinants in cases of child abuse and neglect are (1) parental history and characteristics, (2) child characteristics, (3) early parent-child relationships, and (4) societal attitudes and environmental stresses and resources. Each will be discussed below.

Parental History and Characteristics

Many people tend to regard child abusers as suffering from mental disorders. The most current thinking indicates that there is no simple connection between clinical diagnosis per se and child abuse and neglect. Steele (1980, 50) wrote; "In general, it seems useful to consider child abuse behavior as a group of abnormal patterns of caretaker-child interaction related to psychological characteristics which can exist concurrently, but quite independently, of any psychiatric disorder or even in otherwise relatively healthy personalities."

A frequent finding in the histories of those parents who abuse their children is that they were abused themselves (Steele 1980). This generational pattern of abuse is not present in all cases, however (Kaufman and Zigler 1987), although it is often there but not apparent. Some parents may deny their own history of abuse: they may view their own experience of abuse as children as appropriate discipline for their bad behavior; they may fear, even as adults, retaliation from their parents; or they may try to avoid the painful feelings associated with the abuse they suffered. It is likely that in many instances the parents' early abuse affected their personality development, limited their empathic abilities with their own children, and set the stage for a replay of the abusive environment (Steele 1980, 52).

Why do so many parents fall prey to this generational pattern of abuse? Therese Benedek's (1959) view of the parenting process helps to explain this. Each parent relives his or her own childhood in the process of parenting. The memories of being a child and of how one was parented are reactivated. Parents identify both with their parents and with their experiences as children. Many parents have certain strengths or environmental supports that enable them to rework their own pasts in more positive ways as they raise their own children, making parenting a developmental growth process. Other parents become victims of their own negative childhood experiences and repeat the past.

A second feature in the backgrounds of many abusive parents is a history of an early disturbance of attachment to their own parents that influences the bonding process to their children (Ainsworth 1980). While factors such as complicated deliveries and illnesses during pregnancy may influence parent-infant attachment, for some parents their own early experiences determine the ways they relate to their children.

A third important parental factor in child maltreatment cases is the parents' lack of self-esteem and unresolved developmental needs that predispose them to inordinate stress and frustration in their parenting role (Eldridge and Finnican 1985). Such parents are particularly vulnerable to needing their children to give them approval and meet their needs. The parent generally lacks empathy for the child as a separate being with needs and unique capacities. If the child fails to gratify the parental need or does not meet the parental expectations, then the parent's own infantile rage may be mobilized, resulting in physical abuse. Such rage may also emerge when the child reenacts the "bad" aspects of the parent. Alternatively, the parent may deny certain of the child's needs and neglect may ensue.

A fourth crucial parental factor linked to child maltreatment is alcohol and drug abuse. In a study of two-hundred families with an alcohol- or drug-addicted parent, 22.5 percent of the families either physically or sexually abused their children. All of the children studied suffered from some degree of neglect (Black and Mayer 1980). It also has been noted that such abuse can lead to fetal distress (Lipson 1982) and that fetal alcohol syndrome, resulting from a mother's chronic drinking during pregnancy, had been reported as the third leading cause of birth defects.

Among other parental traits that have been associated with child abuse are: heightened anxiety, aggression, dependence, and lower succorance scores (Egeland, Breitbucher, and Rosenberg 1980); a negative reaction to pregnancy, a lack of knowledge about parent-child relations, and anxiety and fears that interfere with the meeting of parenting demands (Brunnquell, Crichton, and Egeland 1983); impulsivity (Rohrbeck and Twentyman 1986); and a child-management-skill deficit involving a lack of understanding about good child-rearing techniques (Kelly 1983). These characteristics, in combination with other life stressors, seemed to predispose parents to abuse their children.

Parental characteristics are also extremely important in child neglect. A mother's overall level of ego functioning (defined as maturity) has been identified repeatedly as related to the adequacy of child care (Polansky et al. 1981; McCabe 1986). In several studies of low-income neglectful mothers, Polansky identified two types of "infantile" characters: the impulsive and the apathy-futility types. The mothers demonstrating the apathy-futility syndrome showed the following traits: (1) a pervasive belief that nothing is worth doing, (2) emotional numbness characterized by massive affect inhibition, (3) interpersonal relationships characterized by desperate clinging, (4) lack of competence in many areas of living, (5) the expression of anger in passive-aggressive forms and through hostile compliance, and (6) verbal inaccessibility to others, a related crippling in problem solving, and the ability to transmit, largely unconsciously, a sense of futility to those involved with them. Neglectful mothers, in contrast to non-neglectful mothers, also showed less social participation, family support, going out, and lower intelligence; they reported feeling more socially isolated and alienated and less likely to seek help from the community.

Child Factors

The child's own behavior and characteristics may play a role in the abusive act. Steele (1980, 67–68) described "high risk" children who seemed prone to be abused and neglected. He included in this group children who are born following a difficult pregnancy or delivery, at an inconvenient time, or at a time of crisis or high stress for the parents; illegitimate children; those of the "wrong" sex; those born prematurely; and those born with congenital deficiencies, abnormalities, or perinatal illness causing frequent or prolonged hospitalization. He also described children who are "difficult" by virtue of being hyperactive, fussy, hard to feed or cuddle, irregular in their sleeping patterns, or who cry incessantly. Faller and Ziefert (1981, 43–44) noted similar factors, but also observed that active infants are more at risk for abuse while passive infants are more at risk for neglect. They found that among older children, provocative behavior such as aggression, stealing, sexual acting out, or truancy seemed to call forth abusive parental responses. It is difficult, however, to determine whether certain child characteristics that seem associated with abuse are the cause or the effect of the abuse.

Early Parent-Child Relationships

Parental and child characteristics often interact in instances of child abuse in what has been called "a dynamic process of interchange" (Zimrin 1984). For the abused child, deficits in basic trust, self-confidence, self-esteem, affectionate response, and control of aggression are important factors. For the parent, feelings of inadequacy and disappointment in the face of a child's handicap or behavorial problems as well as the symbolic meaning the child has for the parent are crucial. Likewise, there appear to be "spiral effects" (Ainsworth 1980) that can be observed in instances of child abuse. For example, abused children may engage in behavior that is aggressive, distancing, and provocative, thus eliciting even more potential for abuse. In one study (Ainsworth 1980), mothers who were unable to respond to their infants' crying in the first few months of life were more likely to have babies who cried more later on. These children, in turn, were at high risk for later abuse.

Societal Attitudes and Environmental Stresses and Resources

There are societal and environmental factors that contribute to child abuse and neglect. Societal attitudes toward violence set the stage for abuse (Gil 1975). While physical force as a means for disciplining children is not condoned as much as it was previously in American society, television programs and feature films that portray and glorify violence and sadism enjoy enormous popularity and commercial success. Every day millions of individuals are exposed to acts of extreme cruelty and aggression through the media.

Life stress and minimal social supports also are important environmental factors in child abuse. Frustration and situational stress, unemployment, poverty, overcrowding, ghetto conditions, female-headed homes, and the absence of appropriate supports can trigger abusive acts (Gil 1975; Gelles 1973; Navarro and Miranda 1985). Pelton (1978) was the first writer to call attention to the "myth of classlessness" surrounding child abuse and neglect. He cited repeated evidence showing "the hazardous poverty environment" associated particularly with child neglect. He and others (for example, Wolock and Horowitz 1984; Giovannoni and Billingsley 1970) observed that extreme neglect is often found particularly among the "poorest of the poor." Further, neglectful families, in contrast to others, tend to have more children; the parents' own childhood experiences reflect poverty and neglect; the families often have insufficient food, inadequate housing, and a lack of common consumer items such as telephones; and they are more socially isolated from extended family, friends, and the community.

In summary, the causes of child maltreatment are multiple and interactive, involving biological, psychological, environmental, and societal factors. Child abuse and neglect are not psychiatric disorders, although they may occur in individuals who have emotional difficulties. Likewise, child abuse and neglect cannot be equated with parental willful malevolence, although some parents who maltreat their children show hostility and aggressiveness. Parents who are at high risk to commit acts of abuse and neglect have been abused and neglected themselves, have had poor parenting experiences as children, show low self-esteem, and are anxious, impulsive, apathetic, or lack knowledge about and are uncomfortable in their parenting role. Children who show early signs of behavioral problems or physical or emotional difficulties are vulnerable to abuse. Societal attitudes, mores, and laws that encourage violence and physical punishment; poverty; racism; environmental deprivation and stress; social isolation; and the absence of community supports make abuse a more likely outcome. Not all individuals who are subject to these factors, however, maltreat their children. Nor do all children at risk become victims of abuse and neglect. Thus while we have important hypotheses about the causes of child maltreatment, it seems evident that there is not just one type of abusing or neglectful parent or family. A broad-based assessment of the factors that have led to child maltreatment and individualization of the often-interlocking factors in any given instance are crucial to an integrative clinical practice perspective with this population.

How Do We Prevent and Treat Child Abuse and Neglect?

Many treatment approaches have been recommended for work with child maltreatment cases, but there are no clear criteria or guidelines for selection of one approach over another. Research in this area is still in its infancy (Gerbner, Ross, and Zigler 1980).

How one defines a problem will influence largely how one decides to work with it. Thus if one views child maltreatment as having psychological roots, it is logical to select a psychodynamic treatment model. Or, if one focuses on the sociological causes of abuse and neglect, it makes sense to use environmental interventions to advocate for social change. In contrast, if one views the causes of maltreatment as multifaceted, it seems essential to select an approach or a combination of approaches from a broad range, including the psychological, educational, behavioral, or environmental, depending on the needs of particular maltreatment cases. The approaches that have been recommended for work with this population will be reviewed briefly here and will be discussed and illustrated in more detail in later chapters.

Individual Modalities

While individual treatment has often been equated with psycho-dynamically oriented psychotherapy, it also encompasses social-learning and cognitive-behavioral approaches that are more educational in nature. The rationale for a psychodynamically oriented psychotherapeutic treatment approach is based on the view that abusing and neglectful parents themselves suffer from severe personality deficits that impair their parental functioning and predispose them toward child maltreatment. Intervention therefore must aim at ameliorating these core deficits. While concrete and environmental services might be used along with psychotherapy in order to engage the client, to relieve stress, to meet realistic needs, and to promote social supports, such services alone would not be sufficient to alter the potential for maltreatment.

Psychodynamically oriented proponents (Polansky et al. 1981; Blumberg 1977) believe that it is essential for parents to have corrective emotional experiences with "a good parent," to receive emotional support and empathy, and to be exposed to positive role models. These experiences will enable the parents to enhance their self-esteem, to repair ego deficits, to develop empathy for their children, and to learn new ways of dealing with their children and with their lives. Steele (1980, 65), for example, a proponent of a psychodynamically oriented approach, argued that the programs for enhancing parental skills, to the degree that they are successful, are so because of the emotional support and approval provided rather than solely because of the technical skill imparted.

The rationale for the social-learning (Kelly 1983) and cognitive-behavioral (Barth 1985) approaches is based on the view that abuse and neglect are learned behaviors and that attitudes from the past can be modified in the present through the teaching of new interpersonal and self-management skills. The social-learning and cognitive-behavioral theorists feel that it is possible and less time-consuming to produce attitudinal and behavioral changes this way rather than by more traditional psychotherapeutic means. Both approaches attempt to train parents in positive child management techniques and to expand parents' nonviolent repertoires. They promote better means of anger control and more adaptive child management skills and parent-child interactions, and they decrease life-style risk factors such as unemployment.

Family Modalities

Family systems theory views symptoms in any individual member of a family as reflecting family dysfunction. Thus one aims at improving family functioning rather than or in addition to individual functioning. If child maltreatment is to be understood in this light, it is essential to assess and work with the family as a whole, or with selected subsystems, in many instances. A family assessment, for example, might uncover a marital problem that is playing a crucial role in the abuse cycle (Beezley, Martin, and Alexander 1976), faulty communication processes that lead to acting out rather than verbalization of feelings (Wells 1983; Maidman 1984), or disturbed parent-child interactions (Beezley, Martin, and Alexander 1976).

There are a variety of family interventive models, with different aims: modifying what seems to be entrenched family pathology stemming from the parent's own families of origin; improving dysfunctional communication and interactions in the present; changing problematic family roles and structure; teaching the family better management skills; improving the family's connection to social supports; and providing needed services.

Group Modalities

The use of groups in work with child maltreatment cases has received increased attention in recent years. Group approaches tend to be divided into those that are educational, self-help oriented (such as Parents Anonymous), and more traditionally psychotherapeutic. It is noteworthy that existing research data support the efficacy of Parents Anonymous groups in contrast to group therapy in reducing the propensity for future abuse and neglect (Cohn 1979, 517; Faller 1981, 72).

Parent education, provided in a group setting, is a relatively new form of intervention (Elkin 1986). Such a group may teach parenting skills and developmental concepts that can enhance the parents' understanding of their children. Parents are taught how to control their childrens' behavior and to consider the impact of their behavior on their children. Such groups also may contain a socialization component, which seems to be quite important in helping parents to reduce social isolation and in providing emotional support.

Parents Anonymous groups are modeled after those used in Alcoholics Anonymous. They do not have an educational focus per se but instead offer a forum where abusing and neglectful parents help each other to share their feelings and concerns, to confront difficult problems, and to obtain emotional support. Such groups also tend to decrease social isolation.

Child Intervention

Given the need to protect abused and neglected children, it should be no surprise that the most usual form of intervention with the abused or neglected child directly is foster care (Jones and Botsko 1986). Whether foster care or other types of institutional placement for such children are beneficial or harmful is a controversial issue (McQuiston and Kempe 1986; Mann and McDermott 1983). Most abused and neglected children do not receive other types of direct treatment or special intervention (Cohn 1979; Mann and McDermott 1983; McQuiston and Kempe 1986), irrespective of whether they remain in or are placed outside the home.

The decision to place a child outside the home is a serious one that has many implications for both the child and family. Some of these include the feelings generated by the separation, ranging from parental guilt to further scapegoating of the child; disruption of the community relationship for the child; the stigma of placement; loss and grief for the child and family; attachment and dependency which get interrupted; and the potential difficulty in "fitting" back into the original family system (Pipitone and Maidman 1984, 266). Whether out-of-home placement works for the child and his or her family depends on the type and consistency of intervention the family receives during the period of separation and whether there is improvement in the family's ability to care for the child adequately after placement (McQuiston and Kempe 1986).

There are other forms of direct intervention that can be used with children (McQuiston and Kempe 1986; Mann and McDermott 1983). The nature of the interventions should be determined by the child's age and developmental needs. These range from mother-infant stimulation in infancy to day care in early childhood to play therapy and other forms of intervention for the school-age youngster. Play therapy enables children to express their feelings and fantasies through action rather than words alone and has been advocated for all maltreated preschool and early school-age children with emotional problems, unless such treatment mobilizes parental rage that endangers the child (Mann and McDermott 1983). Such children often demonstrate certain ego deficits around impulse control, object relations, and reality testing that can be worked with in play therapy.

Lay Services

Lay therapists usually are nonprofessional volunteers or paid workers, often parents themselves, who are assigned to assist clients with their daily needs (for example, budgeting and transportation to appointments). Often they teach parenting skills and provide emotional support. One exemplary program (Gray and Kaplan 1980) selected lay therapists having the capacity for empathy, flexibility, and high self-esteem. The aides worked in the home, assessed family needs, referred the family for services, provided the family with needed health information and general information on child development, and served as a role model and a "lifeline" at times of stress and crisis. They were available in person or by telephone seven days a week, twenty-four hours a day, and were paid minimum wages. These aids often were experienced as less threatening than professionals, and their use was contraindicated only when parental pathology was so severe as to overwhelm the lay therapists (Beezley, Martin, and Alexander 1976).

Concrete Services

The use of concrete services may be both desirable and necessary in conjunction with all of the other interventive approaches to maltreatment cases outlined here. Families who abuse and neglect their children often lack essential provisions and community supports that can ensure a decent standard of living and provide them some relief from stress. Crisis nurseries, day-care centers, housing assistance, food stamps, and medical and homemaker services are only a few of those services from which families may benefit. In addition, it may be essential to engaging and helping such families that workers demonstrate concrete helpfulness in doing for and assisting clients in their daily lives.

Multipronged Approaches

Child abuse and neglect cases may require a creative combination of approaches. Some authors (Mouzakitis and Varghese 1985) have recommended interventions that simultaneously address (1) the personality traits of the parents, (2) environmental stresses, and (3) the characteristics of the children that make them vulnerable to victimization. They suggest that services must be coordinated, of high intensity, continuous, and involve follow-up. Further, they should be *multidimensional,* being directed at the various components of family functioning; *multidisciplinary,* involving professionals and workers from a variety of disciplines; and *multimodal,* offering a combination of approaches.

Research on Effectiveness

Studies of the outcome of interventive approaches with child maltreatment cases are rare, and those that do exist have been fraught with methodological problems. The most comprehensive study in this area involved a three-year evaluation of eleven federally funded national demonstration programs targeted at child maltreatment cases in the United States and Puerto Rico (Cohn 1979). The study population included 1,724 adults who received treatment for at least one month during a two-year period (1975–76). On average, treatment occurred weekly and lasted six to seven months. Individual treatment, case management, group treatment, lay services, and Parents Anonymous groups were utilized. The study did not point to a single most effective interventive method. Those parents who received lay services as part of their treatment package, however, showed greater improvement than those who did not. During the course of the study, 30 percent of the parents studied were reported to have abused or neglected their children, while 60 percent did not. Parents with a history of previous abuse or neglect and those who experienced a range of stresses that seemed to trigger the maltreatment were more likely to be found in the reincidence group. Parents who did not abuse drugs or alcohol and child abusers, rather than child neglecters, were viewed as less likely to show maltreatment in the future. The best predictor for the reincidence of maltreatment was the severity of the reported abuse or neglect at the time of intake. Reincidence was lowest when highly trained workers were used.

Only three projects in the study provided intervention specifically to children. Of the seventy children studied, all were found to show some dysfunctional behavior, with 70 percent manifesting problems with peers. Over half of the sample had difficulty dealing with frustration, showed poor attention span, and had self-esteem and identity difficulties. Treatment appeared to be helpful to some and not to others.

This chapter has presented an overview of the definition, incidence, causes, and treatment of child abuse and neglect. The major implications of this review for clinical practice point up the need for (1) a broad-based and individualized assessment of child maltreatment cases that encompasses parental personality characteristics, family functioning, environmental stresses, concrete needs, social supports, and sociocultural variables, (2) an empathic, creative, and flexible use of interventive modalities based on the differential needs of a particular case, (3) a broad range of practitioner roles both with the client directly and with the environment, and (4) a clinical research component in which treatment outcome and process can be studied. The next chapter will outline the elements of an integrative clinical-practice perspective that can guide work with this difficult population.

References

Ainsworth, Mary D. Salter. 1980. Attachment and child abuse. In *Child abuse: An agenda for action,* ed. George Gerbner, Catherine J. Ross, and Edward Zigler, 35–47. New York: Oxford University Press.

Barth, Richard P. 1985. Beating the blues: Cognitive-behavioral treatment for depression in child maltreating young mothers. *Clinical Social Work Journal* 13 (4): 317–28.

Beezley, Pat, Harold Martin, and Helen Alexander. 1976. Comprehensive family oriented therapy. In *Child abuse and neglect: The family and the community*, ed. Ray E. Helfer and C. Henry Kempe, 169–94. Cambridge, Mass.: Ballinger.

Benedek, T. 1959. Parenthood as a developmental phase: A contribution to the libido theory. *Journal of the American Psychoanalytic Association* 7:389–417.

Black, Rebecca, and Joseph Mayer. 1980. Parents with special problems: Alcoholism and opiate addition. In *The battered child*, 3d ed., ed. C. Henry Kempe and Ray E. Helfer, 104–13. Chicago: University of Chicago Press.

Blumberg, Marvin. 1977. Treatment of the abused child and the child abuser. *American Journal of Psychotherapy* 31 (2): 204–15.

Brunnquell, Donald, Leslie Crichton, and Byron Egeland. 1983. Maternal personality and attitude in disturbances of child rearing. *American Journal of Orthopsychiatry* 51 (14): 680–98.

Cohn, Anne Harris. 1979. Effective treatment of child abuse and neglect. *Social Work* 24 (6): 513–19.

Egeland, Byron, Mary Breitbucher, and Deborah Rosenberg. 1980. Prospective study of the significance of life stress in the etiology of child abuse. *Journal of Consulting and Clinical Psychology* 48 (2): 195–205.

Eldridge, Amy, and Mary A. Finnican. 1985. Applications of self psychology to the problem of child abuse. *Clinical Social Work Journal* 13 (1): 50–61.

Elkin, Judith. 1986. Parent education in child welfare. In *Child abuse and neglect*, ed. Ronald E. Cohen, Maryann McCabe, and Victor Weiss, 359–77. New York: Office of Projects Development, Appellate Department, Supreme Court.

Faller, Kathleen C. 1981. Resources for intervention. In *Social work with abused and neglected children*, ed. K. Faller, 68–78. New York: Free Press.

Faller, Kathleen C., and Marjorie Ziefert. 1981. Causes of child abuse and neglect. In *Social work with abused and neglected children*, ed. Kathleen C. Faller, 32–51. New York: Free Press.

Frude, Neil, ed. 1981. *Psychological approaches to child abuse*. Totowa, N.J.: Rowman and Littlefield.

Gelles, Richard. 1973. Child abuse as psychopathology: A sociological critique and reformulation. *American Journal of Orthopsychiatry* 43 (4): 611–21.

Gerbner, George, Catherine J. Ross, and Edward Zigler, eds. 1980. *Child abuse: An agenda for action*. New York: Oxford University Press.

Gil, David. 1970. *Violence against children*. Cambridge: Harvard University Press.

———. 1975. Unraveling child abuse. *American Journal of Orthopsychiatry* 45 (3): 346–56.

Giovannoni, Jeanne, and Andrew Billingsley. 1970. Child neglect among the poor: A study of parental adequacy in families of three ethnic groups. *Child Welfare* 49: 196–204.

Gray, Jane, and Betty Kaplan. 1980. The lay health visitor program: An eighteen month experience. In *The battered child,* 3d ed., ed. C. Henry Kempe and Ray E. Helfer, 373–78. Chicago: University of Chicago Press.

Hampton, R., and E. Newberger. 1985. Child abuse incidents and reporting by hospitals: Significance of severity, class, and race. *American Journal of Public Health* 75 (1): 56–60.

Jones, Mary Ann, and Michael Botsko. 1986. *Parental lack of supervison— Nature and consequences of a major child neglect problem.* New York: Child Welfare League of America Research Center.

Kaufman, Joan, and Edward Zigler. 1987. Do abused children become abusive parents? *American Journal of Orthopsychiatry* 57 (2): 186–92.

Kelly, Jeffrey. 1983. *Treating child-abusive families: Intervention based on skills training principles.* New York: Plenum Press.

Kempe, C. Henry, F. N. Silverman, Brandt Steele, W. Droegemueller, and H. K. Silver. 1962. The battered-child syndrome. *Journal of the American Medical Association* 181:17–24.

Kempe, C. Henry, and Ray E. Helfer, eds. 1980. *The battered child,* 3d ed. Chicago: University of Chicago Press.

Lipson, A. 1982. Contamination of the fetal environment—A form of prenatal abuse. In *Child abuse: A community concern,* ed. Kim Oates, 42–48. New York: Brunner/Mazel.

McCabe, Maryann. 1986. Child neglect: A research view. In *Child abuse and neglect,* ed. Ronald E. Cohen, Maryann McCabe, and Victor Weiss, 35–99. New York: Office of Projects Development, Appellate Department, Supreme Court.

McQuiston, Mary, and Ruth S. Kempe. 1986. Treatment of the child. In *Child abuse and neglect,* ed. Ronald E. Cohen, Maryann McCabe, and Victor Weiss, 335–57. New York: Office of Projects Development, Appellate Department, Supreme Court.

Maidman, Frank. 1984. Physical child abuse: Dynamics and practice. In *Child welfare: A source book of knowledge and practice,* ed. Frank Maidman, 135–81. New York: Child Welfare League of America.

Mann, Eberhard, and John F. McDermott. 1983. Play therapy for victims of child abuse and neglect. In *Handbook of play therapy,* ed. Charles E. Schaefer and Kevin J. O'Connor, 283–307. New York: John Wiley and Sons.

Mouzakitis, Chris, and Raju Varghese. 1985. Treatment of child neglect. In *Social work treatment with abused and neglected children,* ed. Chris Mouzakitis and Raju Varghese, 268–79. Springfield, Ill.: Charles C. Thomas.

Navarro, Jose, and Manuel Miranda. 1985. Stress and child abuse in the Hispanic community: A clinical profile. In *Stress and Hispanic mental health: Relating research to service delivery,* ed. William A. Vega and

Manuel Miranda, 239–66. Maryland: National Institute of Mental Health.

Newberger, Eli H. 1983. The helping hand strikes again: Unintended consequences of child abuse reporting. *Journal of Clinical Child Psychology* 12 (3): 307–11.

O'Toole, R., P. Turbett, and C. Nalepka. 1983. Theories, professional knowledge, and diagnoses of child abuse. In *The dark side of families: Current family violence research,* ed. D. Finkelhor et al., 349–62. Beverly Hills: Sage Publications.

Pelton, Leroy H. 1978. Child abuse and neglect: The myth of classlessness. *American Journal of Orthopsychiatry* 48 (4): 608–17.

Pipitone, Joseph, and Frank Maidman. 1984. Residential child care. In *Child welfare: A source book of knowledge and practice,* ed. Frank Maidman, 263–87. New York: Child Welfare League of America.

Polansky, Norman A., et al. 1981. *Damaged parents: An anatomy of child neglect.* Chicago: University of Chicago Press.

Rohrbeck, Cynthia A., and Craig T. Twentyman. 1986. Multimodal assessment of impulsiveness in abusing, neglecting, and nonmaltreating mothers and their preschool children. *Journal of Consulting and Clinical Psychology* 54 (2): 231–36.

Steele, Brandt. 1980. Psychodynamic factors in child abuse. In *The battered child,* 3d ed., ed. C. Henry Kempe and Ray E. Helfer, 49–85. Chicago: University of Chicago Press.

Wells, Susan J. 1983. A model of therapy with abusive and neglectful families. In *Differential diagnoses and treatment in social work,* 3d ed., ed. Francis J. Turner, 715–26. New York: Free Press.

Wolock, Isabel, and Bernard Horowitz. 1984. Child maltreatment as a social problem: The neglect of neglect. *American Journal of Orthopsychiatry* 54 (4): 530–43.

Zimrin, Hanita. 1984. Child abuse: A dynamic process of encounter between needs and personality traits within the family. *American Journal of Family Therapy* 12 (1): 37–47

2

Toward an Integrative
Clinical Practice Perspective

Eda G. Goldstein, D.S.W., and
Gladys Gonzalez-Ramos, D.S.W.

Introduction

Maltreatment can be life-threatening. It often becomes chronic and repeats over generations. Its short- and long-term devastating effects create an urgency that is unparalleled. Individuals who abuse or neglect their children can be helped, but the task requires special skills and exerts unique demands on the practitioner. Clients often are in crisis. Workers may carry responsibility for life-and-death decisions affecting children and may face ethical, medical, and legal dilemmas. Families are frequently resistant to treatment efforts and often appear mistrustful, apathetic, or overtly hostile. There still is relatively little literature to guide the practitioner in this area, and agency and professional supports are lacking. It should be no surprise that those who work with this population often feel isolated and overwhelmed.

This chapter will present the major elements of an integrative perspective that can serve as a framework for clinical practice with child maltreatment cases. First it will define an integrative perspective and describe its view of assessment and intervention. It will then discuss the barriers that exist to implementing an integrative perspective in work with child maltreatment cases. It will conclude with a discussion of the role of supervision and staff development in overcoming some of these barriers.

An Integrative Perspective Defined

The following four principles define what is meant by an integrative perspective:

Principle 1. A social work practitioner always begins with individuals or families who have a problem or need and formulates a plan to meet the need or resolve the problem based on an assessment of the client's situation.

Principle 2. Assessment is broad-based and biopsychosocial in nature. It includes the client, the client's total milieu, and the service delivery network in relation to the needs of the client. Problems are viewed within a multicausal field in which present and past experience, personality and family characteristics, life stage, environmental stresses and resources, and social and cultural attitudes and mores interact.

Principle 3. A range of interventive strategies used either alone or in combination can be selected depending on one's assessment of the client. Intervention may be directed to different systems (individual, marital, community, agency, and so on) or to the relationships among them. Practitioners may draw on therapeutic approaches where appropriate, but their clinical armamentarium should include a wide repertoire of helping strategies and roles. These include, among others, those that encompass therapy, education, advocacy, and mediation.

Principle 4. The practitioner ideally should work for change within the agency, community, and society. Because of his or her ability to identify clients' needs, gaps and obstacles in the service delivery system and community, and dysfunctional societal attitudes and policies, the practitioner's role in broader systems change is vital.

Bridging the gap between these four theoretical principles and their practice application with child maltreatment cases is a difficult and complex task, even for experienced workers. It is not possible to give a manual of rules, techniques, and criteria for how and when to do what to whom. An empathic, creative, and flexible approach is essential. Some of the elements that must enter into such an approach will be outlined below and then discussed and illustrated more fully in later chapters.

Beginning Where the Client Is

A social work practitioner always begins by addressing the client's presenting problem. Unfortunately, it is difficult to do this in many child maltreatment cases. Most of these clients have had experiences with social agencies that leave them mistrustful of services and disillusioned about getting the help they need.

Professionals are more likely to be viewed as enemies than as allies. This is so particularly when children have been or are in the process of being removed from the home, when the court is involved, and when parental compliance with services is linked to whether or not the child remains with or is returned to the parents.

The willingness and ability to engage these parents require the worker's empathy with their despair, which often may appear as apathy, hostility, distrust, and noncompliant and provocative behavior. It also requires the worker's ability to recognize and put aside his or her own feelings of revulsion, anger, and pain in dealing with maltreatment cases. For successful engagement to occur, it may be necessary for the worker to go beyond narrow conceptions of the helping role. Entering the client's life space directly by helping with daily routines or negotiating frustrating environmental systems may convey the worker's genuine concern and confidence. These types of intervention can permit the worker to be experienced as accepting, available, and helpful rather than judgmental, distant, and ineffectual.

There are many factors in the agency, the worker, and the client that influence the engagement process. Moreover, the possibility of legal action and media exposure creates intense pressure on the worker to act decisively or defensively in a case. An agency's program may lead workers to emphasize and interpret certain data so that the client's problem can fit the agency's function. If a setting has the power to make recommendations about separation of child and family, it is likely to produce fear and consequently more defensive client behavior. These client reactions, in turn, may be interpreted negatively. If the agency conveys disrespectful and punitive attitudes, this is likely to induce more resistant behavior in clients who already experience low self-esteem, vulnerability, neediness, shame, failure, guilt, and fear. Thus certain client behaviors, such as failed appointments, defensiveness, hostility, and low motivation, may be assessed as characterological when in fact they are at least in part reactive to the reality of the situation. Similarly, the ease of access, the flexibility of appointment times, and help with transportation or child care and other practical arrangements may affect the client's ability to use services and thus may affect the worker's assessment of the client's motivation. Further, as pointed out by one author (Goldstein 1984, 207) "Cramped, poorly lit, and dirty waiting rooms; rude and insensitive personnel; lack of sharing of important information; unavailability or lack of access to professional staff; and blaming or demeaning attitudes . . . and practices that convey that the client is unable to think for himself, to act rationally, to understand his own or other's problems or conditions, and is an object to be manipulated, controlled, or changed are inimical to the client's ability to be a collaborator in the helping process."

The worker's level of knowledge and skill, values and attitudes, personal characteristics and life stage, reactions to the client, and reality pressures and stresses are important factors in the engagement process. On the most obvious level, the beginning worker may be unprepared for the onslaught of intense feelings that are evoked in attempts to help this population. Even more experienced practitioners who are unused to home visits, for example, may suddenly feel vulnerable and unsafe in unfamiliar and unprotected surroundings, removed from the agency setting. They too may become overwhelmed by their reactions to extreme abuse and neglect and may find it difficult to refrain from judging, punishing, or distancing attitudes and behavior. Because of the intense neediness of many of these families and the pressure to protect a child's life or future, workers may overextend themselves to the point of exhaustion or may assume unrealistically high expectations of themselves. They may hope for quick and clear results and may be unable to appreciate the small gains made by the client, equating slow progress and inevitable setbacks with failure. Or they may distance themselves and refrain from investing in the family at all.

A Framework for Assessment

Assessment is a complex and crucial aspect of work with child maltreatment cases and is the foundation of all interventive decisions and activity. A distinction needs to be made, however, between what may be called an intake or investigative assessment and an interventive or continuing assessment. In the intake or investigative type of assessment, data are collected that are relevant to the task of determining: (1) whether a case will be accepted, (2) whether a child must be taken out of the home, (3) whether the court needs to be involved, and (4) whether and where the family should be referred for services (Mouzakitis 1985a, 187). This phase can be defined as "the process by which the validity or nonvalidity of the reported maltreatment is determined and an initial understanding of the children, the parents, and their situation is acquired that may lead to protective action" (Mouzakitis 1985a, 190). In the interventive or continuous assessment, there is a more comprehensive effort at understanding the major reasons for the current abusive or neglectful behavior, which can serve as a basis for an individualized treatment approach.

While in principle both types of assessment might occur simultaneously and might be carried out by the same individual or team, the usual practice, particularly in urban areas, is to separate the investigative function from the ongoing service function. The investigative assessment is particularly difficult because of the crisis nature of many of the cases, their seriousness and potential threat to life, and the inevitable intrusiveness and threatening nature of the diagnostic process with involuntary clients who have been reported for abuse and neglect. Its focus has to be selective and immediate in determining the seriousness of the case, the parent's motivation and ability to provide adequate care and protection, the effect of the maltreatment on the child, and the services that can be utilized to help ensure the child's safety and care.

It is beyond the scope of this chapter to consider fully the nature of investigative assessment and the related issues of out-of-home placement and/or court involvement. A more detailed discussion of this topic can be found in chapters 6 and 9. In all phases of work with child maltreatment cases, however, there is a need to assess whether or not the parent or parents are able to act in the best interests of the child's safety and well-being. It has been suggested that in abuse cases, the worker focus on the following in order to make this determination (Mouzakitis 1985b, 220):

1. whether the parents, through their actions and behaviors, are able to control aggressive and hostile impulses toward the children;
2. whether the parents recognize (directly or indirectly) their abusive behavior;
3. whether the parents verbalize and show evidence that they want to work with the agency;
4. whether the children show no evidence of further abuse.

In neglect cases Mouzakitis (1985b, 220) further suggested that one consider:

1. whether the parents provide adequate supervision;
2. whether the parents provide adequate medical care;
3. whether the parents provide adequate food and clothing;
4. whether the parents make sure the children attend school;
5. whether the parents provide adequate housing;
6. whether the parents show evidence of improving their childrearing skills;
7. whether the overall emotional atmosphere in the home is conducive to the children's normal growth;
8. whether the parents demonstrate their ability to use community resources to the children's and their own welfare;
9. whether the parents demonstrate their desire to work with the agency.

These criteria are relative and subjective, however, and do not address some of the more subtle and vexing questions that the practitioner may have during the interventive process. For example, when does parental improvement in child management skills indicate that the parent will not resort to physical abuse under stress? When does parental verbalization of wishes to injure children, as part of discussing their feelings and stresses during the course of treatment, border on loss of impulse control? When does the absence of a worker or other caretaking person (through illness or vacation, for example) who stabilizes the family threaten the ability of the parents to protect and care for the children? This is an extremely complex matter for which there are no simple or exact guidelines.

The interventive or continuous assessment process begins with the identifying data; the referral source; the presenting problem, including the severity of the child abuse or neglect; the history of the current difficulties; and the history of past difficulties. The assessment then should gather data regarding the child, the parental personality(ies), the family system, the social environment, and the interrelationships among these four areas. The chart offered here shows a framework for a full biopsychosocial assessment in child maltreatment cases. It is intended as a guide to the important areas of attention rather than as a precise set of issues to be covered in a systematic fashion.

Areas of Assessment in Child Maltreatment

The Parental Personality(ies)

1. Sociocultural background and values
2. Life-cycle stage and needs
3. Ego functioning and coping mechanisms
4. Self-esteem
5. Developmental accomplishments and difficulties
6. Social functioning
7. Background including history of abuse and/or neglect
8. Knowledge and values regarding child development and child management
9. Special problems (emotional or physical illness or disability)
10. Impact of and attitudes toward abuse and/or neglect
11. Self-awareness, motivation, and expectations
12. Past experiences with helping agencies
13. Impact of separation from child

The Family System

1. Financial and other material resources (housing, living conditions, etc.)
2. Life-cycle stage and needs
3. Child management practices
4. Roles and structure

The Child System

1. Life-cycle stage and needs
2. Physical condition
3. Ego functioning and coping
4. Developmental accomplishments
5. Social functioning

The Family System (*Cont.*)

5. Communication
6. Interpersonal relationships
7. Coping strategies
8. Social Integration

The Child System (*Cont.*)

6. Special problems or risk factors
7. Impact of abuse and/or neglect
8. Impact of separation from family

The Social Environment

1. Stresses
2. Rewards
3. Societal values, policies, and attitudes
4. Available resources
5. Service delivery network

The purpose of collecting this data is to gain a fuller understanding of the case in order to plan treatment. In organizing the data, it is important to consider the following questions:

1. To what extent is the maltreatment a function of stresses imposed by current life roles, developmental tasks, situational stress, or a traumatic event?
2. To what extent is the maltreatment a function of parental impairments in ego functioning, developmental difficulties and dynamics, or special problems?
3. To what extent is the maltreatment a function of the child's idiosyncratic characteristics or problems?
4. To what extent is the maltreatment a function of a lack of fit between the individual's or family's needs and essential knowledge and/or resources?
5. To what extent is the maltreatment shaped by sociocultural factors?
6. What individual and/or family capacities and strengths and environmental resources can be mobilized to prevent further maltreatment and to improve individual and family functioning?
7. Given the client's level of motivation and expectations, attitude toward services, and past experiences with helping agencies, what interventive strategy would best engage the client at this time?

8. What interventive strategies would fit best with this client in order to achieve long-term results?

The answers to these questions help the practitioner to choose a treatment approach. It is likely that most acts of child maltreatment are a function of the interaction among all the factors. In many instances however, the maltreatment may appear to stem from a specific combination of them. Some approaches are better suited to addressing one type of difficulty than another.

This framework for assessment, when applied to actual case situations, may seem unrealistic and unattainable. The actual assessment process in child maltreatment cases usually cannot be accomplished through traditional means. Individuals who abuse or neglect their children may not be able to come to one's office and sit and talk at appropriate times and in a focused way. It will probably be necessary to enter the parents' world not only in terms of home visits but also through participating in the parents' daily routines. Observing the family members through sharing in their activities may be the main way in which crucial assessment data are obtained. For example, one may observe whether daily routines are structured or chaotic, how money is managed, whether the children are appropriately dressed, how food is prepared, and so on. Such observations can provide vital clues about the parents' level of ego functioning, capacity for empathy and responsiveness, methods of discipline, the nature of environmental stresses, and the resources available to meet important needs. Such direct observation affords the worker a creative opportunity to "be where the client is" and to prioritize interventions according to the immediate needs of the family (Gonzalez-Ramos 1987).

Selecting a Treatment Approach

The goals of intervention may be short-term or long-term. They should aim at dealing with the current crisis, engaging the client in the helping process, and preventing further abuse and neglect. In many of the child maltreatment cases, it may not be possible to implement an optimal long-range plan immediately. The client's hopelessness, lack of motivation, distrust, overwhelming life situation, or lack of resources may need to be addressed first. Doing whatever is necessary to engage the client is the first priority after securing the child's safety and well-being. It has been suggested, for example, that the provision of concrete services, in addition to meeting client need, also may be a means of showing the client that the worker or agency wants to help. Similarly, helping the client to make some type of small desired change in his or her life may also be a way of gaining trust. If the parent or family is more motivated to accept help, it may be possible to involve them in treatment approaches that are more directly focused on dealing with the abuse or neglect problem.

There are many possible treatment approaches that can be used with child maltreatment cases. Among these are various types of individual, family, and group modalities involving therapy, education, behavioral and cognitive approaches, and self-help; concrete services and work with the environment; the use of lay services such as homemakers; play therapy and other direct work with children; out-of-home treatment such as foster care; and agency, community, and social change.

In selecting a particular modality it is important to consider not only the goals of intervention but also the client's particular characteristics. Thus, if it seemed desirable to try to improve a client's parenting skills, one could utilize any of the three modalities of individual, family, or group treatment, but other considerations may make one approach preferable to another. For example, some parents might feel less threatened by a group and would benefit from the mutual support, sharing of ideas, and identification with other parents. Other parents might assimilate knowledge about child development and management better when they are individualized and nurtured in a one-to-one relationship. Still other clients might learn best from the modeling of good parenting skills in situations, for example, in which homemakers or other caretaking persons assist the client in the client's home.

Once an approach is selected, goals should be partialized. This will help the worker and client to feel less overwhelmed and discouraged in the face of such difficult problems as well as enable greater focusing, monitoring of progress, and appreciation of the client's often small steps toward change. Many of the capacities that workers may take for granted at the beginning of their work with other clients may be hard to achieve even after a great deal of intervention with mal-treating parents. In many instances, for example, it can take a long time to help clients get to the point where they can identify and verbalize their feelings toward their children. Likewise, the client's willingness to see the worker on a regular basis or to reach out to the worker in a crisis is not a criterion for beginning a case but rather the hard-won result of helping efforts.

In order to provide an individualized array of services to clients who abuse and/or neglect their children, multiple agencies and work-ers often need to be involved. This generally leads to fragmentation and problems in the coordination and collaboration that is so essen-tial to successful treatment. Alternative service models that provide a variety of services through one umbrella setting, for example, might enable more flexibiliy and coordination and thus more effective inter-vention with this population. Another possible model would be the use of multidisciplinary or multiagency teams (not just teams within a setting) that are coordinated across agencies.

Practitioner Roles and Use of Self

Empathy, flexibility, and creativity are essential to success in maltreatment cases. Empathy involves the ability to put oneself in the shoes of clients and to understand them from "inside," so to speak. It does not mean condoning behavior. It does mean that one attempts to understand what it feels like to be the client and what the client's subjective experience of himself or herself, others, and the world is. It involves being able to tune in to what the client feels even if the client cannot express his or her feelings directly. It requires listening to and sharing the client's pain and other strong feelings. It means being able to put aside a desire to defend oneself, others, or the agency, or to tell clients what is good for them, or how they should behave. At the same time it does not mean that one doesn't act to set limits on potentially violent or destructive behavior or that one refrains from taking actions to protect clients. This dual requirement—to be em-pathic and to protect—is one of the most difficult aspects of work with child maltreatment cases. In some instances it may not be possi-ble to do both simultaneously and to maintain a viable client-worker relationship. In other instances, setting limits and protecting the clients from themselves may be a form of empathic responsiveness.

Flexibility and creativity in using oneself require the worker to let go of certain fixed roles with clients in favor of others that may be unfamiliar, uncomfortable, and of less professional status. Outreach is a key component of engaging clients in maltreatment cases, often in the face of their attempts to convince workers that they want no part of them. Persistent efforts to be useful in their lives will pay off. "The 'talking cure' oftens turns clients off initially. It raises their anxiety and seems futile. Entering the client's world through doing often is viewed more favorably. Using a 'hands on' technique to show parents alternative ways of dealing with children, when done in a non-judgmental way, can be helpful" (Gonzalez-Ramos 1987). The client-worker relationship then can be experienced nonassaultively, as a safe and helpful "holding environment" for the client (Dougherty 1983).

Practitioners also have a vital role in identifying and working to remedy gaps in and barriers to the agency's or community's ability to serve clients. In being on the front-line in work with their clients, they are in optimal positions to see the gaps and obstacles to service that exist and to collaborate with others in order to effect agency and social change. This requires different skills from direct work with clients. The assessment of the organizational context in which services are delivered and the ways of negotiating in order to produce systemic change are not subjects ordinarily taught to practitioners. Nor does the agency system or society at large view the worker's "change agent" role as desirable. The worker may feel that he or she lacks not only the skill but also the power to effect such change. Moreover it may seem and, in fact, be threatening to one's position or status to try "to change the system." Workers need to equip themselves for this crucial practice role.

Overcoming Barriers to Effective Intervention

There are numerous barriers currently to implementing effective intervention in the child maltreatment area.

The issue of whether or not to intervene in child maltreatment cases is influenced by often conflicting societal values. For example, one's outrage at violence directed against children and wish to protect them may clash with one's sensitivity to the rights of parents to rear children without interference in ways that are consistent with their cultural and personal belief systems.

Establishing effective services at the institutional or program level is very demanding. Meeting client need often calls for highly flexible arrangements involving evening appointments, twenty-four-hour emergency services, day care, transportation, other concrete services, and considerable staff time spent in advocacy. Many of these services are nonrevenue-producing and involve time-consuming, draining, and frustrating activity. Further, in an atmosphere of malpractice claims and media pressure, administrative and staff concern about lawsuits may lead to self-protective rather than clinically sound choices in working with child maltreatment cases. A recent article defined the latest mental health professional's syndrome as "litigaphobia," a condition brought on by excessive worry and a feeling of being under seige in the atmosphere of malpractice claims (Turkington 1986, 1).

Work with child maltreatment cases often involves multiple agencies (for example, legal, welfare, mental health, and medical) that are not coordinated and that sometimes work against one another, sometimes inadvertently and at times because one setting depreciates the work of another. This splitting of the agencies into "good" and "bad," together with lack of coordination and communication among involved settings, recreates the problems in families themselves (Whiting 1977). In many instances agencies and workers view maltreatment cases quite negatively, experience them as being "dumped," and reject or transfer the case to another setting or worker. Such clients are often "screened out" rather than "screened in" (Maldonado 1986).

At the practitioner level, the pressures of work with child maltreatment cases are enormous, especially when such cases constitute a large percentage of one's caseload. Practitioners may be caught, for example, between a desire to protect the child and a conviction that removing the child from his or her family is punitive and wrong. They may feel repugnance at the ways children are treated, wish to rescue them, and/or have difficulty empathizing because the parents' intense loneliness and depletion may stir up similar feelings in themselves. Anger and feelings of rejection can be elicited in a worker who is verbally attacked by the client, and disappointment and feelings of inadequacy, futility, and failure may arise when clients show abusive behavior or continue to neglect their children. Practitioners may be fearful of the client's potential for violence and of crime-ridden residential areas. They may be overwhelmed or repelled by the neediness, emotional deprivation, and dependency of the clients or by the physically deteriorated and economically impoverished conditions in which clients live. Practitioners may withdraw from, reject, or overinvest in clients to overcome feelings of helplessness and hopelessness in the face of enormous unfulfilled needs.

Dedication, a high level of skill, and a supportive agency milieu are vital to the practitioner in this field. In many instances, however, inexperienced workers are assigned the most difficult cases, and often agencies lack support groups, educationally oriented supervision, and staff development programs that provide opportunities for workers to share their work and learn from one another. While clients need consistency and long-term supportive services and relationships, they experience high worker turnover and burnout.

Some important coping mechanisms noted in successful practitioners are:

1. having the ability to stay in touch with one's feelings about one's clients;
2. having a guiding theory for the work to be done;
3. having worked through in one's personal life some of the problems likely to be encountered in clients' lives;
4. having some hopeful cases in one's caseload; and
5. having the feeling that one is becoming more competent in one's work (Polansky et al. 1981, 242–44).

Practitioners also need to find ways of releasing tension and "refueling" in order to maintain their level of positive involvement in their work.

The Role of Supervision and Staff Development

Agency supports are crucial in equipping workers with the knowledge, skills, and help essential to providing effective intervention and to combating staff turnover and burnout. Cohn (1983, 204–5) described burnout in the maltreatment field as occurring when "the worker is unable to provide clients with the support, guidance, and energy necessary to ensure a successful course of treatment." The First National Evaluation Study of Child Abuse and Neglect Demonstration Programs (Cohn 1983, 205–6) looked at organization and management factors as well as the workers' personal characteristics that contributed to a positive work setting (as opposed to one producing burnout). This study of 162 workers in eleven programs revealed that workers were less likely to show burnout if, within the context of a structured, supportive environment, there also existed strong and supportive leadership, clear communication, worker involvement in decision making, and room for innovation. Burnout was also less likely to occur when the workers' caseloads were smaller and they were more experienced.

One important source of worker support stems from the way services are structured (for example, the use of interdisciplinary teams that share work, decision making, and responsibility; mutual aid; smaller caseloads; and flexible work schedules). Supervision and staff development programs can play crucial supportive roles. Following Kadushin (1985), some agencies have experimented with separating the administrative and educational aspects of supervision, with each presumably having supportive aspects. This model has advantages because it designates time to be used specifically for learning that is less likely to be encroached upon by workload pressures. Workers may also feel more open with a supervisor to whom they are not directly accountable administratively, and the agency can assign the most knowlegeable (but not necessarily the most administratively oriented) staff to teaching roles. This model also allows for more flexibility for staff to take on gratifying assignments who might not be able to move into the few administrative supervisory slots that exist. In addition, separating the administrative and educational functions permits the use of group or peer supervision, models that may be helpful in enhancing mutual sharing, aid, and cohesiveness.

A systematic staff development program that contains didactic, experiential, and expressive elements complements supervision. Such a program should involve a combination of lectures, discussion groups, assigned readings, role plays, case seminars, and the use of audiovisual aids. Optimally such a program should be graduated so that experienced workers are trained in more advanced principles. Such opportunities also provide much-needed "breathing space" and allow for more relaxed social and staff "nurturing" activities.

There are several important content areas that a staff development program should address: (1) information regarding policies, laws, and regulations, entitlement and welfare programs and their eligibility requirements, and community resources, and (2) theoretical knowlege and practical skills training in understanding, engaging, and working with maltreatment cases. Content on cultural diversity and its impact on personal and family values, childrearing practices, and attitudes toward the use of services is crucial, as are opportunities for discussion of moral and value conflicts, countertransference feelings, and work stresses.

Another aspect of a sound staff development program involves encouraging workers to write about their work or to make presentations of successful and/or challenging work to others, both within and outside the setting. In addition, it is important to provide opportunities for workers to learn about new professional developments and to build or maintain connections to others in the professional community through attendance at meetings and conferences or through taking courses outside of the setting. These are important sources of renewal and stimulation.

This chapter has presented an overview of the major elements of an integrative clinical practice perspective in work with abused and neglected children and their families. It has concluded with a discussion of the barriers to implementing effective intervention and the role of supervision and staff development in overcoming some of these barriers. The following chapters will discuss and illustrate in more detail the practice principles and techniques that can be used in work with this population.

References

Cohn, Anne H. 1983. The treatment of child abuse: What do we know about what works. In *Child abuse and neglect: Research and innovation,* ed. Jerome E. Leavit, 195–209. Boston: Martinus Nijhoff, Publishers.

Dougherty, Nora. 1983. The holding environment: Breaking the cycle of abuse. *Social Casework* 64 (5): 283–90.

Goldstein, Eda. 1984. *Ego psychology and social work practice.* New York: Free Press.

Gonzalez-Ramos, Gladys. 1987. Overcoming the barriers to intervention. Speech delivered at New York University Symposium on Child Abuse and Neglect, April 10.

Kadushin, Alfred. 1985. *Supervision in social work,* 2d ed. New York: Columbia University Press.

Maldonado, Miguelina (Chairperson of the New York Hispanic Task Force on Child Abuse and Neglect). 1986. Telephone interview, December.

Mouzakitis, Chris. 1985a. Intake—Investigative assessment. In *Social work treatment with abused and neglected children,* ed. Chris Mouzakitis and Raju Varghese, 187–204. Springfield, Ill.: Charles C. Thomas.

———. 1985b. Continuing assessment. In *Social work treatment with abused and neglected children,* ed. Chris Mouzakitis and Raju Varghese, 205–25. Springfield, Ill.: Charles C. Thomas.

Polansky, Norman, et al. 1981. *Damaged parents: An anatomy of child neglect.* Chicago: University of Chicago Press.

Turkington, Carol. 1986. Litigaphobia. *American Psychological Association Monitor,* Nov. 1986.

Whiting, Leila. 1977. A community multi-disciplinary child protection team. *Children Today* 6 (1): 10–12.

3

Individual Treatment

Judith M. Mishne, D.S.W.

Introduction

Individual treatment is the most frequently used modality in work with abused and neglected children and their parents. It can be used with a wide spectrum of clients and can be flexibly provided in a myriad of ways, including crisis intervention, short-term, long-term, ego-supportive, intensive or ego-modifying, educative, and cognitive behavioral. Individual treatment is also useful in conjunction with a variety of other types of supportive and concrete services. This chapter will present a view of individual treatment that is consistent with an integrative approach to social work practice with maltreatment cases. It will define individual treatment and suggest criteria for its use. Different types of individual treatment will be considered and selected principles of intervention with adults and children will be presented and illustrated. The chapter will conclude with a discussion of important issues and new directions in work with abused and neglected children and their parents.

Definitions

As discussed in chapter 2, there is general consensus that parental personality traits, life stress, and environmental and cultural factors must be considered in selection of an appropriate treatment approach. The choice of intervention must be based on an assessment

38

of the biopsychosocial factors that have led to the infliction of injury upon children by parents or caretakers.

Individual treatment encompasses a broad range of interventions aimed at restoring, maintaining, and enhancing the individual's personal and social functioning. A traditional nondirective and insight-oriented individual approach limited to the psychological treatment of emotional problems is rarely useful in maltreatment cases. Along with newer psychotherapeutic approaches that emphasize ego building, the enhancement of self-esteem and mastery, the development of interpersonal empathy, and the acquisition of better child management skills, it is important to utilize concrete services and other types of environmental supports. In addition, both crisis-oriented multidisciplinary outreach and long-term rehabilitative approaches are commonly necessary. Comprehensive and coordinated treatment efforts must include, as needed, therapy, education and guidance, day care, homemaker services, Alcoholics Anonymous, drug programs, telephone crisis hotlines, and parent aides in a broad, integrated approach that entails an "orchestration of community facilities" (Thurston 1980).

Criteria

The decision to recommend individual treatment should emerge from an individualized case-by-case assessment process. As described in chapter 2, this diagnostic endeavor must include a systems perspective to provide an appraisal of the strengths and weaknesses in both the client and the helping network. Even if individual treatment were the optimal choice, it should be recommended only when available within the helping system. Some programs rely heavily, even exclusively, on case management efforts. These programs use referral approaches to link up families with existent community services, including day care, parent hotlines, support groups, and so forth, and do not use more "therapeutic" or educative types of treatment. Others provide purchase-of-service contracts with local child-serving agencies, such as mental health services and child guidance clinics, which provide individual treatment.

Individual treatment can help parents:

1. to enhance ego functioning, particularly in the areas of impulse control and judgment;
2. to acquire better coping skills;
3. to develop the self-esteem and empathy that are so essential to good parenting;
4. to improve role functioning and interpersonal relationships;
5. to learn better child management techniques;
6. to develop more realistic and age-appropriate expectations of children;
7. to modify long-standing behavior patterns;
8. to compensate for early developmental arrests;
9. to gain greater self-awareness;
10. to improve relationships with the community.

Some clinicians have erroneously viewed persons who are poor or of minority backgrounds as inaccessible to clinically oriented treatment approaches—a clearly invalid stereotype (Spurlock and Cohen 1969). Many of these individuals who have suffered childhood deprivations, neglect, and abuse repeat these patterns with their own children. They need to be engaged for a substantial period with a worker in the privacy and safety of the one-to-one therapeutic relationship. In addition to providing other supportive services where necessary to improve the client's functioning, the worker can serve as a role model and "corrective" parental figure who can help the parent to resume the developmental growth process and become capable of improving parental skills.

In most situations, individual treatment is the preferred approach for a variety of reasons. Working with family violence puts the worker under special pressures. Equal support to the child and the parent is difficult, if not impossible, in family sessions. Each member of the system needs empathy and support in order to make something more than an unwilling and tenuous connection. Group therapy for some clients causes more acute disturbance, resulting in acting-out behavior. Sometimes clients who feel ashamed, humiliated, and guilty cannot tolerate public self-exposure and can be open and revealing only in the privacy of a one-to-one confidential contact. Groups can be very threatening to individuals overly sensitive to criticism. Some fragile clients are too easily affected by the other members in the group.

Frequently, mandates from protective services prohibit contact between parents and children, making it necessary to see family members individually. Sometimes both parents cannot be engaged until a crisis occurs as, for example, when a father's terror at the prospect of losing his children and his wife breaks down his resistance to treatment. Practical problems can arise that may make it difficult to implement other approaches. In many cases, it is difficult initially for abusive and neglectful parents to keep routine office appointments for themselves and their children. Thus lateness, failures, cancellations, and impulsive rescheduling interfere with maintaining traditional family and group sessions. The need for home visits, crisis intervention sessions, continual availability in between appointments, and for securing additional special programs such as homemaker services, shelters for battered women and their children, day care, and so forth, requires the consistent involvement of a committed and flexible worker.

The decision that a particular individual or family is "unworkable" or "untreatable" must be made with great caution and only after reasonable efforts have been made to engage the family. Kempe and Kempe (1978, 68) referred to a group of abusive parents, about 10 percent of the total, who were too disturbed to treat. They recommended an end of the parents' "caregiving relationship by placing the child with relatives or in permanent foster care, or by adoption." The untreatable population they described consists of four groups:

1. parents who suffer delusional psychosis, in which the child as a symbiotic extension of the parent is a part of the delusional system and hallucinatory commands to kill are directed against the child, cannot be treated;
2. aggressive sociopaths, explosive and violent individuals, many of whom are commonly alcohol- and/or drug-addicted, incapable of control, cannot be trusted to parent their children;
3. parents who are cruel and openly sadistic, engaging in torturous punishments of children over minor infractions, such as bedwetting, ineptness, and so forth, are not amenable to treatment while children are in the home;

4. seriously mentally ill "fanatics," employing extreme religiosity to justify their autocratic, idiosyncratic views of "crime and punishment," are inaccessible to treatment, as they hold tenaciously to their beliefs and are impervious to other perspectives.

Types of Individual Treatment with Adults

While they may overlap, there are four main types of individual intervention in work with adults: ego-supportive, intensive or ego-modifying, education and guidance, and cognitive-behavioral. While they will be described separately below, they must be used flexibly in work with individuals who have abused or neglected their children.

Ego-Supportive Treatment

Ego-supportive treatment aims at restoring, maintaining, or enhancing the individual's adaptive functioning as well as strengthening or building ego where there are deficits or impairments (Goldstein 1984, 153). It may be short- or long-term in nature and use both psychological and environmental interventions. The focus of ego-supportive treatment generally is on here-and-now behavior, reality pressures, current relationships, conscious thoughts and feelings, and states of need and vulnerability. There may be some selective focus on past experiences as they directly relate to the present. Ego-supportive intervention with parents who abuse or neglect their children aims at better control of behavior and feelings, improved parent-child and other interpersonal relationships, and better coping skills. In some cases there are efforts to remedy early parental developmental defects that may be a part of the abuse/neglect pattern. The client-worker relationship is critical in order to foster acceptance, sustain the client, increase motivation to change, develop empathy and self-esteem, permit role modeling, and promote corrective experiences. The provision of information, advice, and direction is used in supportive intervention in order to help parents acquire greater understanding of their own and their children's needs and better ways of managing their own and their children's impulses and behavior. Many supportive concrete services are required in addition to in-the-office treatment for parents and children. Home visits may be necessary during the engagement period, as an indication of outreach and to show that something must be done whether or not parents cooperate.

Intensive or Ego-Modifying Treatment

Ego-modifying treatment aims for some reconstruction of the personality. The examination of inner conflicts is undertaken to understand what has gone awry. This level of work requires a client with the following characteristics: introspection and psychological open-mindedness, a long-term commitment, a high level of motivation, an ability to verbalize rather than act on intense feelings, a strong enough ego to tolerate the upheaval that results from stirring up highly charged issues, and an absence of unusual or severe environmental pressure. These characteristics generally are not in evidence in parents who abuse or neglect their children, particularly in the early stages of treatment. Attempting such treatment too early, or even at all in some instances, may make matters worse. There are individuals, however, who can benefit from such an approach when it is done skillfully.

Education and Guidance

While education and guidance can be used as part of an individual ego-supportive approach as well as in family and group modalities, they also can be the primary techniques used with parents who abuse or neglect their children. Much abusive behavior erupts out of parents' feeling helpless and overwhelmed by a fitful child or one who is difficult to feed, toilet train, and so forth. Education and guidance can help parents alleviate anxiety, promote more realistic expectations, develop greater understanding and empathy for the child, and foster a greater sense of mastery and self-esteem. Factual information can help parents understand child development, childrearing techniques, and special problems. It also is important for parents to learn about their own needs and impulses and ways of managing these better. Parents can be helped to examine the consequences of different actions. The goal is to improve the child's milieu by bolstering parents' confidence and helping them function more comfortably in the role of parent.

Cognitive-Behavioral Treatment

This form of treatment aims specifically at controlling anger and other types of destructive behavior, changing specific behavioral sequences that contribute to abuse and neglect, and improving child management skills. It is an active and directive approach that is reality oriented. It does not address the underlying causes of abuse and/or neglect but attempts to influence and change problematic behavior in the here-and-now.

The Treatment of Children

Direct individual treatment of children is a crucial but often neglected dimension in maltreatment cases. The type of intervention that is appropriate depends on the child's age, developmental needs, problem severity, and the ability to verbalize, as well as the availability of external support. Child treatment can help repair damaged self-esteem, promote ego functioning and age-appropriate behavior, and stimulate growth. Treatment can include both verbal and play techniques as well as concrete types of intervention.

In play therapy childhood trauma are relived in a warm and supportive environment. Whenever an experience or event is too difficult or too large to assimilate it must be reworked, over and over, to allow for a passively experienced one to be converted into an actively experienced one. "In children's play, the more favorable condition lies in the fact that the play apparently is under control of the child. Further reassurance is formed in the reversal of roles. The child often in imagination or in acted-out play takes on the powerful part, while assigning the weaker, more passive or suffering role to a toy, a pet, or another . . . thereby reenacting in an active way, what he had previosly experienced passively" (Greenacre 1959, 64). Play is the avenue or road to understanding a child's affects, defenses, traumas, relationships, wishes, and hopes.

Selected Treatment Principles and Techniques with Adults

The Importance of Empathy

After the child's relative safety and health are ensured, the treatment of the parent is the first priority (Kempe and Kempe 1978). Generally parents who maltreat their children do not view their behavior as problematic or painful. Even if they do become anxious or upset over their acts of abuse or neglect, they often feel hopeless and mistrustful of authority, sometimes with good reason. They also lack insight, have difficulty verbalizing their feelings, and do not value talking as a means to problem-solving. Because many maltreated child cases are nonvoluntary—mandated by police or departments of child welfare—parental resistance is high.

Empathizing with the clients' feelings regardless of the destructiveness of their behavior is important in all phases of work with maltreated children and their parents, but it is crucial to successful engagement in treatment. The therapeutic alliance results both from the client's readiness to accept help and from the worker's ability to mobilize the client's hope, trust, and willingness to work on difficult problems. Thus the worker must make every effort to empathize with parental fears and needs and to convey respect for any positive parental efforts made to cope with their lives. It is important to move beyond seeing the abused or neglected child as the helpless victim of "bad" parents, to seeing parents also as victims of their own troubled pasts and current stresses.

Empathy is the feeling that emerges, enabling clinicians to sense their clients' emotions and penetrate "their screen of defenses (and symptoms) which often hides their real feelings" (Olden 1953). It is very difficult to empathize with abusive parents because of the fear and revulsion they commonly elicit. Additionally, their moods and explosive outbursts can bewilder workers. The key to empathy with such parents is the deepest possible understanding of their past. This requires that clinicians work with their clients and themselves, and in a sense live in two worlds—the past and the present, the real and unreal, their own and someone else's simultaneously. The empathic understanding of abusive parents evolves as the worker enters into their stressed and frightening world of today simultaneously with entering into their past, namely, the parents' childhood, so that a link is made between the violence they commonly endured before and the violence they now demonstrate against their own youngsters.

Selma Fraiberg emphasizes the importance of remembering as the key to helping save parents from the blind repetition of their morbid past. Through remembering, they can identify with and empathize with themselves as injured children and thereby empathize with their own children. If they cannot be helped by the worker to make this link imaginatively, they remain tied to the fearsome figures of their past, repeatedly inflicting that past on their children.

The following case example shows the worker's efforts to relate empathically to the fears underlying the client's so-called resistance to involvement in treatment. The worker promoted the client's ventilation of her problems and offered support. She was accepting and conveyed a feeling of respect for the client. Advice was not offered, since the mother felt battered by good advice.

Ms. C., a thirty-three-year-old woman of mixed racial background, was referred to an urban child guidance clinic for an evaluation of her nine-year-old daughter, Mary, who did not work at school, refused to talk or respond appropriately to peers or her teachers, and, on increasingly numerous occasions, had wild temper tantrums in class and on the playground. Because of ever-changing teachers and substitutes, the school did not refer her for help. Ms. C. sought help for herself and her daughter from a medical social worker, following her own repeated hospitalizations for hypertension. The mother had shared some of her concerns and anxieties about her child with the hospital social worker, who described the mother as resistant and ambivalent, procrastinating about seeking services for herself and her daughter. The mother recognized that diet and medication were of little avail and finally accepted the medical findings that her health crisis and panic states were due to stress and anxiety. She was "fearful" of any form of psychological treatment.

When the new worker who was assigned to Ms. C. met with her for the first time, she quickly acknowledged what a "handful" Mary was and that she wanted to be of help to Ms. C. in whatever way she could. She said that she knew how difficult it was to be a parent. Ms. C. answered that she was in a frenzy about Mary, who had been late one hundred times, refusing to leave the playground and enter the school, playing with matches, swearing, and generally being noncommunicative. At home Mary would play school and do pretend workbook assignments only for her mother, not her teacher. Ms. C. was in an agitated state and kept her children up until midnight to try to help them with their schoolwork and to get them to do their homework. She often whipped Mary, in an attempt to get her to comply and cooperate. The worker wondered if this had been done to Ms. C. when she was small, and Ms. C., with surprise, said yes. The worker commented that such methods never worked and were in fact painful to both parent and the child. The worker commented that she could see that Ms. C. really cared about raising Mary right and that it must seem so frustrating and overwhelming when Mary did not respond. Ms. C. nodded and said cautiously that she wasn't expecting the worker to understand. The worker then said that sometimes parents have a lot of concern that they will be blamed and punished for their behavior and that they often don't want treatment. Ms. C. revealed her terror that she would not prove to be an adequate mother. She feared this might result in her children being taken away. Thus, her initial resistance to the referral for help and her frenzied physical brutality to her children, expecially Mary, in an effort to make them conform and perform could be understood in a sympathetic light. The worker's empathy helped to form a trusting alliance with the client.

As Ms. C. began to accept the worker's genuine concern, she began to share more of her fears and concerns. The worker was able to help Ms. C. relax by saying things like: "I'm so glad that since we met, you've been able to keep your appointments regularly, which has helped us both sort out what's been going on at home." "I know how tense and ill you've been, and this has made you often very worried and fearful about your children." "Of course you don't want to lose your children" "After your own unhappy childhood in an institution, you'd prefer that your children were raised together, at home with you." "I hope that gradually, as we work together, you'll become more at ease with me, and realize our goal is to work together to improve things at home, and not take your children away." "Yes, at this clinic we have seen other children like Mary, and I feel confident that our joint efforts can greatly improve Mary's school work and ability to talk and interact outside your home." "I can help you understand some of Mary's worries, and with time, show you ways of discipline and support that will not frighten you or your daughter."

Once she found she could relax in an unthreatening and supportive atmosphere, Ms. C. proved to be open and accessible. Without any threat of losing her child or being judged badly, she was heartened by the worker's respect for her concerns, understanding attitudes about the origins of her excessive physical discipline, and reassurance that soon new, more effective parenting skills would be discussed and shared in their ongoing contact.

The Use of Authority

In many situations, abusive and neglectful parents will not seek help unless forced to do so. The use of authority to motivate parents to seek help must be followed by firm but sensitive interventions by the worker in order to convert the parent's compliance to real motivation and engagement. The following example shows this dual process.

Mr. and Mrs. S., a common-law husband and wife, were called into court after their two-year-old son Kevin sustained a fractured leg while being disciplined by his father. The father gave the toddler a severe spanking, then slammed him to the floor. Kevin was detained at the hospital by the orthopedic resident and security staff; the parents were informed that the mother must move herself and her children away from her husband before Kevin would be discharged. A court hearing was scheduled. The court investigation revealed a common-law marriage replete with chronic violence, including beatings when the wife, Verna, was pregnant, causing a miscarriage. Mr. S. denied the severity of his actions, cited all injuries as accidents, and on the basis of his denial and lack of concern, psychotherapeutic invervention was not recommended. The court was quickly aware of Mrs. S's history of separations from and reconciliations with Mr. S., even at the time when Kevin was in the hospital. Though Mrs. S. (Verna) subsequently moved herself and her children, she reconciled with Mr. S. in a matter of weeks, and the court granted a continuance for ninety days to allow her to establish independent housing, obtain a restraining order, and enter counseling. Mr. S. also agreed to enter counseling. Kevin was detained in special temporary foster care because of his healing leg fracture. The other children, who were in brief temporary care, were released to their mother. She was unsuccessful in securing adequate housing. Since Mr. S. failed to make contact at the Department of Children's Services and did not attend therapy sessions, the protective services worker recommended his visiting be monitored by the agency. He was subsequently imprisoned as a result of a burglary conviction. Court supervision was ordered to assess the ongoing progress by the mother, and to ensure that she continue in treatment and obtain adequate independent housing. It was anticipated that Verna might well reunite with Mr. S. upon his release from prison or, given her history, seek another violent substitute for him. The worker underlined the legal reality that Verna and her common-law husband could lose parental rights of their children if they did not seek treatment and make the necessary changes in their lives.

In her first meeting with the new worker, Verna seemed superficially compliant. The experienced worker commented on how trapped Verna must feel, being made to seek treatment and to remain separated from Mr. S. under the threat of losing her children while at the same time feeling pulled by her attachment to him. When Verna nodded and became silent, the worker said that right now it was true that Verna was in a bad spot and that it would take time for her to feel that she had some options. The worker added that it was not her intent to force Verna to do something she did not feel able to do, but that she wanted to try to help her feel better about herself and to take more control of her life. Verna began crying and said angrily, "No one gives a damn about me, why should you? All you people have done is cause me trouble." The worker said that she could understand Verna's distrust and feelings that treatment might make matters worse. "You have had to do a lot for yourself so far with very little help." Verna said that the only one who had helped her was Mr. S. She knew he was "bad" but she did not know how to get along without him. The worker said that perhaps they could work together on how to help make it easier for Verna to manage with Mr. S. in prison. She added that this was the first priority, and reassured her that she did not have to promise more than she felt able to right now. Verna seem to relax. She began to talk about her living arrangements, which were dreadfully inadequate. The worker and she began to explore options that Verna had with respect to housing.

Help with the Decision to Relinquish Parental Rights

In some instances children require foster care, other types of placement, or adoption. Clearly it is preferable for the parents to make this decision themselves rather than to have it imposed upon them. This is a delicate matter. Even in instances where the parents have severely abused or neglected the child and are unable to provide adequate care, they may be unable to relinquish custody.

The following example shows the worker's efforts to help the client arrive at the decision to place her child up for adoption.

Ms. A. was referred to the Juvenile Protective Association by the child protective service unit of the Department of Children and Family Services. A report was made to this department by a local hospital based largely on Ms. A.'s behavior prior to her daughter's admission and during her stay in the hospital. In a rage, Ms. A. threw a bottle at a male nurse in the emergency room because he wanted her daughter admitted. She made statements, over-heard by the staff, that she could kill her daughter and no one could do anything about it because it was her baby. Because of Ms. A.'s behavior, hospital staff were concerned that the multiple depressed skull fractures for which the child was being treated were a result of deliberate injury by Ms. A. rather than consequent to an automobile accident, as Ms. A. had stated.

Ms. A. was born in a large urban setting in the midwest. She was abandoned at age three, "left in the alley in a trash can." She did not adjust well to placement. School was an unpleasant experience, both because Ms. A. had learning disabilities and because she was severely punished for not getting top grades. Ms. A.'s childhood memories include her foster mother making her sit on a stove burner for wetting her pants, knocking out her front teeth with a cast iron frying pan for talking back, locking her in a closet for what Ms. A. remembers as three or four days as punishment, locking her in a dark cellar with her sister, and deliberately breaking Ms. A.'s arm when she was seven or eight. Ms. A. also reported that she was raped by a foster brother.

At age ten or eleven, Ms. A. ran away from her foster home. She remembers being psychiatrically hospitalized for about a year and being on a ward with violent older patients whose behavior terrified her. She also recalls violent episodes in which she threw furniture at attendants, and being held in restraints on numerous occasions.

Ms. A.'s first pregnancy was at age seventeen; the child, a boy, was stillborn. She married the father of this child and later gave birth to a girl. When her daughter was eighteen months old Ms. A. lost both her job at a fast food franchise and her apartment. She went to an agency for help and they convinced her to put her daughter up for adoption. Her husband, from whom she was divorced, refused to allow it and gained custody of the child despite the fact that he had not assisted Ms. A. in caring for her, and in fact had abandoned them both to live with another woman.

Shortly after, Ms. A. met her second husband, a man who had recently been released from prison, where he served time for armed robbery. He was physically abusive to her and, according to Ms. A., broke her jaw and cracked her ribs. She said that when she told him she was pregnant, he kicked her in the stomach repeatedly and deserted her. Ms. A. had another daughter from this husband.

When Ms. A. was first referred for treatment, Anna was in foster care. Ms. A. felt guilt-ridden about having abused and "rejected" her daughter. She felt she had inflicted the same kind of horror on her child that she had experienced herself. She kept saying in an emotional voice, "I want my child back." The worker was accepting of Ms. A.'s wish to do the best for her daughter but explored in an accepting way the past troubles and current stresses that led Ms. A. to abuse her daughter and place her in foster care. The worker helped Ms. A. to ventilate her anger about the burdens she had faced. It became clear that Ms. A. had never felt able to take care of a child. While she felt her daughter "should be with her, she was able to admit that most of the time she did not want her and found it hard to have positive feelings for her. The worker helped Ms. A. to accept the need to attend to her own needs at this time in her life, particularly in the light of her past deprivations and traumas. She also explored Ms. A.'s feelings about and aspirations for herself and her child. She desperately wanted her child to have opportunities she felt she was denied. These opportunities included being loved and admired. The worker discussed the realities and consequence of the different available options and was able to help Ms. A. recognize her strong wish that her daughter have better opportunities in life. Ms. A. concluded that she did not have it within her to provide for her child emotionally. She decided with the help of the worker to permit adoption.

Help in Breaking the Cycle of Abuse

In some instances it is possible to alleviate the personality difficulties of the abusing parent as a way of breaking the cycle of abuse. This requires many supportive techniques and a strong bond between parent and worker, who offers a "corrective experience" that can ameliorate the effect of the parents' own deprived and traumatic childhood experiences. It also may require helping the parent link his or her own present behavior to past events. The following case offers an example of this type of intervention.

The R. family consists of Mrs. R., twenty-three, and her three children, Steven, six, Daniel, five, and Louise, three. When the juvenile protective services became involved with the R. family, they were supported by public assistance and living in a condemned building. Mr. R. had left the family a year earlier. Mrs. R. had severely beaten her son Steven when he needed to be punished. She had hit him twice with a stick, causing bruises and a laceration on his buttocks. Although Mrs. R.'s explanation for the beatings was to punish Steven for poor school performance, it soon became apparent that the reasons for the beatings reached far back into the mother's earlier relationship with her son and indeed into her own early childhood. Mrs. R. was referred for in-home counseling so that the problem between her and Steven could be assessed and treated.

The assessment revealed that Mrs. R. had herself been abused as a child and witnessed terrible fights between her parents. When these fights occurred, there was no adult to help Mrs. R. with the emotional trauma she experienced. This left her distrustful of both her own feelings about herself and the feelings of others towards her. This sense of uncertainty about herself led her to the misuse of drugs and alcohol as an adolescent, to an unwanted pregnancy at fifteen, to marriage with a man who frequently abused her, and ultimately, to her severe abuse of her first child, Steven.

Tragically, Steven's history had already begun to repeat his mother's. At age two, Steven was abandoned by his mother and placed by the Child Protective Agency in the care of his grandmother for the next year and a half. While Steven was away, Mrs. R. married and stabilized her life so that DCFS returned Steven to her care. After his return, Steven was at times terrified as he witnessed terrible fights between his mother and stepfather. Emotionally and psychologically Steven began to suffer the same painful feelings that his mother had long ago endured, but not forgotten. Because she could not face this, she literally would try to beat these feelings out of him.

The worker tried to develop a relationship with Mrs. R. in which she could feel safe to relive some of her earlier feelings of being mistreated as a child and to use the worker as a benign parental figure who would be attuned to her needs in ways that she had not experienced previously. The worker tried to relate empathically to Mrs. R.'s needs and life experiences, offering sustainment for Mrs. R.'s efforts to make a life for herself. After a long period of testing, Mrs. R. developed a trusting relationship with the worker, and was able to confide in her. With the worker's help she was able to gain control of her abusive impulses. The worker helped Mrs. R. obtain a tutor for Steven and located a special after-school program for him to attend. Slowly and patiently over a two-year period, Mrs. R. relived and examined her early childhood experiences and the emotions that she had never dared to feel or express directly, but that lived on in her relationship with Steven. She gained considerable relief from the treatment process and her self-esteem grew. She became better able to empathize with Steven and to see him as a separate and distinct person. During the final year of treatment the worker helped Mrs. R. focus more on bettering herself. She helped her to identify and consider school and work options and supported her through her attendance at secretarial school.

When Mrs. R. ended her involvement with her agency worker, she had markedly improved her life and she had not beaten Steven since the referral for treatment. Steven's school performance had improved dramatically. There was no abuse of the younger children. The family also located better housing and Mrs. R. had completed secretarial school and was actively seeking employment.

Selected Individual Treatment Principles and Techniques with Children

Parental Involvement

In some situations children can begin in therapy following an assessment, prior to the regular assignment of a worker to the parents. Very disturbed parents, however, commonly cannot tolerate the prospect of the child's receiving help while they do not. Jealousy and siblinglike rivalries with their children abound in abusive homes, as parents are reminded of the neglect, abuse, and rejection of their own childhoods. When the child is in treatment, parents can be competitive and jealous of their child's emerging private relationship with his or her worker. Parents may need considerable contact with their child's worker or their own worker to overcome their fears and resistances, or they may need to be assigned to the same worker in order to maintain their attachment to their child, guard family secrets, and avoid fears of loyalty conflicts, until such time that separation is less threatening.

Preadolescent children generally cannot benefit from therapeutic efforts that do not include contacts with parents. However, when parents' fears are overwhelming—as is commonly the case with those forced to comply with an edict to secure treatment—it rarely helps to sidestep parents and work with the child alone. If the child is seen for an hour or two a week, little can be accomplished unless simultaneous changes in the home support the child's therapeutic gains. Children are generally unwilling to discuss freely their difficulties with their workers. When a child does speak of being abused, it poses special problems. If the revelations do not result in behavior shifts by the parents, the worker can be viewed as still another helpless adult unable to offer safety and protection.

Child Therapy

Play has traditionally been employed as a diagnostic and treatment modality. Acting and playing out unconscious material and real-life events enable a child to share, relive, reenact, test reality, and sublimate, thereby improving ego functions. With abused children, such enactments are often the only access to the child's traumatic experiences and subsequent fears. Using a nonverbal mode the child can "tell" the worker what has happened and/or what keeps happening. Loyalty conflicts, shame, and self-blame for parental abuse are common reactions in abused children. Thus, what cannot be "told" can possibly be played out or depicted in drawings and painting. Art work and play of abused children can clearly reflect "helplessness, powerlessness, fragmentation, depression, anger, and anxiety" (Wohl and Kaufman 1985, 135).

Play, drawings, and enactments are the primary vehicles in the treatment of younger clients, but in some cases the child cannot play, but rather presents an impoverished state and manifests agitated affect and anxiety about events in school and at home. Children need opportunity to put troubling feelings into words and help in connecting their actions to disturbing feelings. In many instances limits and structure need to be provided. The worker listens and observes while the child unburdens himself or herself to solicit an ally, an advocate who will act as intermediary, an ombudsman with parents, foster parents, and the court. In some instances the child's worker must take on a case management role to ensure necessary additional services such as tutoring, medical evaluations, and summer camp.

Joy was seen biweekly for a two-year period, beginning at age four and a half. For the first year in therapy, she frequently required limits and restrictions from the worker. For example, in the seventh session, Joy had difficulty entering the office and acted silly and defiant, running about the waiting room. Once in the office, she was most provocative, grabbing at the drapes and darting toward the cabinets and drawers of other children's special toys and drawings, initially ignoring her own drawer. The worker reflected that her problems coming into the office were possibly related to another morning fight with mommy. Joy agreed and blurted out that she had been watching TV when her mother wanted her to wash up and leave promptly to catch the bus. The worker noted that following such fights it always was hard for Joy to say goodby to mommy in the waiting room and to come in for her own appointment. Seemingly ignoring that comment, Joy went to her drawer for drawing material and said she wanted to draw Easter baskets. Her drawing reflected her agitation, and she exploded and kicked the metal desk yelling that the worker didn't help her draw well and that she was leaving to find mommy.

The worker said that she could not run out and that mother was having her own therapy session, but they could phone her if she needed to talk to her now. Joy began to scream and kick and attempted to hit the worker. She was stopped in this and became more and more furious, testing, but not completely out of control. The worker held Joy's hands and told her that she would not let Joy hurt her, herself, or the furniture, and that they would do nothing until she was calmer. She shouted back that the worker should shut up, that she would have a tantrum and would get her way. She struggled, kicked, swept the dollhouse off the shelf, and tried to bite the worker and leave the office. The worker pushed her chair against the door to stop Joy from dashing out and held Joy in her lap, facing outward to avoid her attempts to bite and spit. The worker told her that she realized this was just like the scary fights at home that she and mommy had told her about, which always ended up with mommy giving Joy a severe spanking and telling her that she was giving her away to a foster family.

The worker assured Joy—still writhing, but listening attentively—that she wasn't angry, and that this kind of upset was one of the most important problems for them to work on. The worker indicated that, in her office, she was in charge and no one would be hurt. Joy yelled that she would tell her grandmother on the worker, and that she wanted to go to an office where the worker wasn't in charge. After some minutes, Joy gradually became calmer, absorbed the reality of the situation, and said she was okay and would clean up the room. She wanted to phone mommy. The phone call was followed by a quick visit to the office where mommy was being seen. Joy reentered her worker's office looking very relieved (that mommy hadn't left her) and went to play with the doll house, where she constructed "a mommy and little girl having fun making dinner together and not angry anymore." When the worker reflected on their working on these fights and struggles together, her serious response was, "Maybe I should come here every day."

Once Joy's acting out had diminished, she could relax in treatment, play more constructively, and articulate her feelings of loneliness and her desire for a normal family life. She did many dramatizations and role plays of a mother and daughter and made construction-paper costumes and props (such as hats, purses, and jewelry) to complement her scenarios. At times, she cast the worker into the role of mother, older sister, or school peer.

Treatment also included contact with Joy's teachers and regular educative and supportive help to her mother. The mother was helped to become a more consistent, empathic parent and was better able to understand Joy's alternating behavior patterns.

Confidentiality

Confidentiality is a major controversial issue in individual work with parents and children. Frequently, a one-way policy of confidentiality is used: that is, "children should know that the content of their sessions will not be revealed but that they are entitled to know what the parents discuss" (Mishne 1983, 245). Abusive parents often try to deny, conceal, or censor their children's accounts of their home life. Some children cover to protect their parents and/or themselves, out of loyalty and/or fear of reprisal. Workers often are given information about eruptive, frightening situations at home, but are forbidden to discuss these situations with the parents. It is not uncommon that this material may be shared by a child or a mother about the father. It may take considerable time and effort until the worker gains permission to deal with such information. On occasions when abuse is shared, it is such that confidentiality cannot be maintained; and in fact protective custody must be sought on an emergency basis. This cannot be done without a clear explication to the client who gave the information. Handling must be well timed and of such a nature that agency intervention does not endanger but rather protects the abused child or spouse.

The Treatment Relationship

The real relationship between the client and worker, so essential in treatment of children and adults, is based on the client's realistic perceptions of the person and qualities of the worker, and the worker's demonstration of respect, compassion, empathy, and hopefulness. Tyson (1980) noted the nontransferential ways in which the worker's gender, age, physical features, style, and manner affect the relationship in individual treatment. A professional can serve as a new object, a corrective figure, a role model, or a teacher, and all of his or her actual characteristics can provide possible foci for resistance or alliance.

Transference refers to those client reactions to the worker that are based on the client's projections onto the worker of feelings and attitudes that stem from past relationships with significant others, mainly the parents and siblings. Because of the abused and neglected parent's own childhood deprivations and trauma, transference reactions in treatment often create great turbulence. Extreme anger, dependency, and longing are common. A parent may be easily hurt, frustrated, or rejected by the worker's going on vacation, for example. When coupled with a propensity for impulsive acting-out, such reactions may disrupt the treatment or precipitate destructive acts outside of the treatment.

In work with children, the parents are not objects of the past, since the child generally resides or has contact with them. The treatment relationship is "often a complicated mixture of elements of a real relationship, an extension into the treatment of current relationships and a repetition or revival of the past" (Tyson 1978, 213). There are difficulties in keeping separate and distinct the two kinds of relationships, particularly in individual work with children. Most children seen in individual treatment view the worker as an intermediary or ombudsman between themselves and their parents, which can create treatment barriers with children who demand that *their* external world be changed. They may want the worker to take over the parenting role, transform the parents, or reunite or separate the parents. In many instances the children are realistic in looking to the worker with explicit demands that their external world be changed. Genuine treatment with children cannot occur until the child is in a safe milieu.

Abused children described by Kempe and Kempe (1978) commonly manifest compliance and acceptance, hypervigilance, lack of trust, and secretiveness, or demonlike negative, aggressive, hyperactive behaviors. These affects and responses are not transference phenomena per se; rather, they are characteristics commonly demonstrated in many situations—home, school, and in the therapy session. The worker's calm and caring stance is often mistrusted; provocative behaviors test and retest each environment and often provoke in home after home the original trauma, and the cycle of abuse and rejection begins anew. As a result, these children are often moved from home to home.

The distinction between the "real relationship" and the transference relationship is not always clear-cut—as nothing is uninfluenced by the past. Unfortunately, the child's and parents' negative relationship experiences, expecially in situations of maltreatment, will have more effect on the modes "of relating than will the excellent qualities of the positive new object [the worker]. The abused child who has experienced multiple foster homes and disruption in significant ties may not relate meaningfully to the most skilled worker" (Mishne 1983, 269, 270). Additionally, parents who have been abused or neglected themselves will have considerable difficulty trusting a worker's empathy and caring, and may try to provoke the worker to mistreat them.

Countertransference refers to those reactions of the worker that are unprovoked by the client. They are displacements onto the client of feelings and attitudes from the worker's past significant relationships.

Sometimes countertransference refers to all the reactions the worker has to the client (Dewald 1964). Counterreactions, by contrast, are not unprovoked reactions or idiosyncratic unique responses of a given worker. Counterreactions, rather, are warranted by the client's behavior—for example, constant barrages of hostility. These reactions must nevertheless be understood and controlled.

Generally an experienced practitioner can examine and resolve feelings that are aroused by a client in order to facilitate resolution of various therapeutic impasses in cases with very special countertransference and conterreaction problems. Many such cases often arouse anger, fear, revulsion, or denial and rescue fantasies.

In addition to countertransferential overidentification with the child or the parents, there are numerous negative counterreactions and negative countertransference dilemmas with impulsive, acting-out, highly narcissistic patients who tax, provoke, and immobilize workers (Proctor 1959; Epstein and Feiner 1979; Giovacchini 1985; Wallace and Wallace 1985). Counterresistance and counterattack by the worker are common responses, arousing feelings of rejection and blame in the client which need to be worked through.

In recent years an increasing amount of attention has been given to emotional exhaustion, "burnout," and impaired job performance of those engaged in work with child abuse cases. Burnout has been defined as the "extent to which workers have been separated or withdraw from the original meaning and purpose of their work" (Berkeley Planning Associates, 1977). Maslach (1977) observed that the degree of burnout depends on the worker's emotional stress in dealing with very taxing cases, such as clients who are physically and verbally abusive, who suffer overwhelming reality life stress, and who are involved in what is deemed as distasteful or frightening behavior. Others emphasize the agency as a factor producing burnout due to poor communication within the agency, lack of support and adequate supervision, unrealistic demands on the worker, lack of variety and autonomy in the job, impossible pressures and emergency demands for overtime, rigid rules, and bureaucratic policies (Armstrong 1977).

Babcock (1967) noted the special stresses on practitioners engaged in individual treatment of children and parents. Almost universally, children are "captive" nonvoluntary clients, brought by their parents or referred by schools, pediatricians, and an array of medical and social agencies. Individual child therapy calls for extensive collaborative work with parents, schools, camps, child welfare agencies, childcare workers, and so forth. Given these added parameters, work with children and parents is often seen as more taxing than work with self-referred adult clients. In Dewald's view (1964), these problems and stresses can evoke a number of common responses, such as a loss of interest and a defeatist attitude. The special demand of work with maltreated children and their abusive nonvoluntary parents only intensifies the responses.

New Directions

One of the more recent developments has been the growth of community-based flexible comprehensive programs (Maluccio and Marlow 1972; Whittaker 1979; Shyne and Schroeder 1978) that offer a continuum of care in which children and parents can receive the most appropriate level of care without getting lost in the system as their needs change. Broadly based team efforts using experts from many disciplines are required. Kempe and Kempe (1978, 115) noted that in such teams "the social workers are the leaders, assisted, as equal and valued partners, by a team of additional professionals, including a pediatrician, a health visitor, a representative of the police, a lawyer, a psychologist or psychiatrist, and if at all possible, a member of the lay public as well." These authors noted the three distinct phases in management of child abuse:

1. crisis management, which includes diagnosing the family situation and developing a long-term treatment plan for each family member;
2. carrying out those plans;
3. raising the consciousness of other professionals in the community, evaluating the work done, and researching further into the problem and its remedies.

All three of the above phases demonstrate the ongoing need for individualized assessment, individualized treatment, and individualized follow-up and evaluation, case by case, child by child, family by family.

References

Armstrong, K. 1977. How can we avoid burnout? Paper presented at the Second Annual National Conference on Child Abuse and Neglect, April 17–20. Houston, Texas.

Babcock, C. 1967. Having chosen to work with children. Paper presented to the Extension Division of the Child Therapy Program, the Chicago Institute for Psychoanalysis, February 10. Chicago.

Berkeley Planning Associates. 1977. *Evaluation of child abuse and neglect demonstration projects: 1974–77.* Vol. 9. Hyattsville, Md.: National Center for Health Services.

Dewald, P. 1964. *Psychotherapy: A dynamic approach.* New York: Basic Books.

Epstein, L., and A. H. Feiner. 1979. *Countertransference.* New York: Jason Aronson.

Giovacchini, P. 1985. Countertransference and the severely disturbed adolescent. *Adolescent psychiatry, Vol. 12, Development and clinical studies,* ed. S. Feinstein et al., 447–48. Chicago: University of Chicago Press.

Goldstein, Eda. 1984. *Ego psychology and social work practice.* New York: Free Press.

Greenacre, P. 1959. Play in relation to creative imagination. *The Psychoanalytic Study of the Child* 14:61–81.

Kempe, R. S., and C. H. Kempe. 1978. *Child abuse—The developing child.* Cambridge: Harvard University Press.

Maluccio, A., and W. Marlow. 1972. Residential treatment of emotionally disturbed children: A review of the literature. *Social Service Review* 46:230–50.

Maslach, C. 1977. Burnout: A social psychological analysis. Paper presented at the Annual Convention of the American Psychological Association, August. San Francisco.

Mishne, J. 1983. *Clinical work with children.* New York: Free Press.

———. 1986. *Clinical work with adolescents.* New York: Free Press.

Olden, C. 1953. On adult empathy with children. *The Psychoanalytic Study of the Child* 8: 111–26.

Proctor, J. 1959. Countertransference phenomena in the treatment of severe character disorders in children and adolescents. In *Dynamic psychopathology in childhood,* ed. L. Jessner and E. Pavenstaedt, 293–309. New York: Grune and Stratton.

Shyne, A., and A. Schroeder. 1978. *A national study of social services to children and their families.* Rockville, Md.: Westal.

Spurlock, J., and R. S. Cohen. 1969. Should the poor get none? *Journal of American Academy of Child Psychiatry* 8: 16–35.

Thurston, H. W. 1980. *The dependent child.* New York: Columbia University Press.

Tyson, P. 1978. Transference and developmental issues in the analysis of a prelatency child. *The Psychoanalytic Study of the Child* 33: 213–36.

———. 1980. The gender of the analyst—In Relation to transferrence-countertransference manifestations in prelatency children. *The Psychoanalytic Study of the Child* 35: 321–38.

Wallace, N. L., and M. E. Wallace. 1985. Transference/countertransference issues in the treatment of an acting out adolescent. *Adolescent psychiatry. Vol. 12, Development and clinical studies.* ed. S. C. Feinstein, M. Sugar, A. E. Esman, J. G. Looney, A. Z. Schwartzberg, and A. D. Sorosky. Chicago: University of Chicago Press.

Whittaker, J. 1979. *Caring for troubled children.* San Francisco: Jossey-Bass.

Wohl, A., and B. Kaufman. 1985. *Silent screams and hidden cries—An interpretation of art work by children from violent homes.* New York: Brunner/Mazel.

4

Family Treatment

Sue Klavans Simring, D.S.W., and
Judith M. Mishne, D.S.W.

Introduction

A family perspective has historically been fundamental to social work practice. As early as 1922, Mary Richmond observed that the concern of the social worker is all those who share a common table (Richmond 1922). Ever since, professionals have clearly recognized that changes or alterations in one or more members of a family produce effects "on other family members, for better or worse" (Strean 1978, 169). A family systems perspective looks at the individual client and concludes that it is not appropriate in practice to perceive the individual alone as the problem, "but rather to see him as an aching limb or member of a family body whose functioning and balance have gone awry . . ." (Sherman 1974, 461).

When considering intervention on behalf of children, one must have a family perspective. "The child cannot be treated in isolation, independent of the reality of the parents, the home milieu, and the needs of the siblings. Given the child's complete dependency on home and family, the supports or obstacles within the family must be regarded as most significant. This reality changes as the child matures" (Mishne 1983, 206). In maltreatment cases, the entire family system, including nonabused siblings and extended family members, is affected in some way by the abuse or neglect of a child. When the family system is seen as the unit of attention, there is a need to select treatment strategies that will address the family's characteristics and transactions as a unit.

This chapter will define what is meant by family treatment within an integrative practice perspective and will suggest criteria for its use. It will describe different types of family treatment and the nature of assessment and will then discuss and illustrate selected principles and techniques of family treatment with maltreatment cases.

Definitions

Family treatment or family therapy has been defined in numerous ways. The field of family therapy emerged from the idea of conjoint treatment where the entire family or a relevant subunit of the family was seen together, as contrasted with the traditional approach, in which family members were seen individually by the same or different workers. Some theorists, however, define family therapy by its approach and focus rather than by the number of people seen together. Thus Johnson agreed with Gurman's and Kniskern's definition of family therapy as "any psychotherapeutic endeavor which explicitly focuses on altering the interactions between or among family members, and seeks to improve the functioning of the family as a unit, [the functioning of] its subsystems, and/or the functioning of individual members of the family" (Johnson 1986, 299). This definition does not require conjoint family sessions.

While family systems thinking and some type of family-centered intervention are essential in most maltreatment cases, this chapter defines family treatment per se as an approach in which parents and children are seen simultaneously, with an explicit focus on family interactions. Family therapy is only one method of working with families of abused children. It should be used selectively based on a thorough assessment of the family and is generally not appropriate with cases involving severe pathology and/or severe physical abuse.

Criteria

There is considerable controversy about indications and contraindications for family therapy and a paucity of research on the outcome of family treatment with specific populations. Furthermore, there is little published about family therapy with maltreatment cases. Thus a decision whether or not to use family treatment usually evolves out of practitioners' personal preference, training, and experience.

There are numerous advantages to seeing family members together in certain cases of child abuse and neglect. The worker can assess family interaction and the roles family members take with one another. Family treatment can help parents learn to communicate more directly, to problem-solve jointly, to empathize with other family members including the child, and to learn and experiment with more effective child management techniques. Frequently, parents will become less defensive when they feel accepted by a worker who is clearly identified not only with the child. Interactions with parents and children also serve to offer modeling, reassurance, limit setting, and appropriate modes of discipline. The worker's firm structure of the sessions introduces controls to an environment that is diffuse and frightening. Interactions between children and parents can often be soothed and calmed by the worker. Joint sessions may also reduce family members' (and workers') tendency to polarize, split, blame, or scapegoat members of the family system.

We suggest the following criteria as guidelines for offering family treatment initially:

1. The degree of pathology. Treatment of the family in a joint therapeutic approach is feasible and sound when the "children are old enough, the family sufficiently articulate, and [where] the level of anger in it not too high . . ." (Kempe and Kempe 1978, 80). These characteristics describe a functional family system—that is, not too chaotic, and where there exist sufficient bonds of loyalty and attachment.
2. The degree of motivation. In order to use family treatment, clients must have some recognition of difficulties and some willingness to participate in a treatment program on a regular basis. It may still be difficult to engage all the relevant family members in coming to sessions routinely. Practical problems can also interfere with regular attendance. In some situations the entire family is eager and willing to meet, and in other cases, only specific members will convene in joint sessions. Experience has shown that it is counter-

productive and often detrimental to therapeutic efforts to insist the entire family meet together.

3. The availability of treatment resources. Most programs do not offer family treatment. Furthermore, family therapists are usually not experienced in dealing with family violence. Because of its distinctive focus and techniques, family therapy requires specialized training.

Most families in which serious maltreatment occurs are dysfunctional and lack motivation to change. "There are families in which violence, drug abuse, incest, and other serious problems plague the family for protracted periods. One or both parents are often impaired by some form of psychopathology. They rarely have adequate executive capabilities and are frequently overwhelmed by the tasks of parenting and family life" (Weitzman 1985, 474). Even with these families, family treatment may become an option at a later stage in the treatment process. Establishing some balance in the family system or subsystem is crucial in order to engage family members in joint treatment.

Similarly, many families refuse to meet together because of denial of problems, overt hostility to treatment recommendations, suspiciousness, fear, or fragile self-esteem. A stage of interventive work that attempts to engage various family members and to help them achieve some semblance of trust and stability is essential prior to any attempts at family treatment.

Contraindications for family therapy are:

1. severe parental psychosis;
2. explosive, sociopathic, and frankly cruel parents;
3. a history of serious injury to child inflicted by parents;
4. parental mental retardation;
5. parental substance abuse.

Types of Family Treatment

Family therapy aims at four major, somewhat overlapping goals:

1. support of adaptive functioning;
2. help in problem solving;

3. overt behavioral change;
4. modification of systemic family processes (e.g. communication, interpersonal relationships, structure, etc.).

These goals are present in family therapy with all client populations but must specifically relate to the problems of abuse in the treatment of maltreating families.

Support of Adaptive Functioning

This goal, for child abuse cases, refers to the practitioner's supporting instances of good childrearing practices on the part of parents that could help prevent or modify the abuse of the child. For instance, the Myers family, consisting of both parents and two children, revealed the following patterns of abuse. The parents rarely checked out whether the youngsters did their homework or showed concern about how they did in school. When the youngsters brought home failing grades, the parents would become enraged and abusive. However, Mr. Myers mentioned several isolated occasions when he tried to check on the children's homework, showing that there was some concern. The worker encouraged the parents to check the children's homework regularly and to remain informed about their school functioning. At each session, the worker would ask the parents if they had been checking the homework. The worker noticed that if she forgot to ask, the parents forgot to check. If she remembered to ask, the parents remembered to check. In this way, a parallel process occurred in the worker's supporting helpful parental functioning. The worker's checking on the parents led to the parents checking on the children. As the youngsters did better in school, the parents' abusive behavior considerably lessened.

Help in Problem Solving

In maltreating families, members often are not able to solve problems but instead become frustrated, angry, and abusive. The Jones family is an example. Twelve-year-old Marvin complained that he was picked on by his teacher, who never complimented him on his achievements and blamed him whenever any of the boys in his class did anything wrong. Marvin was enraged at the teacher and became increasingly hostile and defiant. Whenever Marvin told his parents what was happening in school between him and his teacher, his father blamed him and would tell him to straighten himself out. Marvin became increasingly arrogant and got into shouting matches with his parents that resulted in the father's beating him.

The worker intervened by having Marvin and his parents listen to one another instead of attacking each other. He asked the parents, "How do you know Marvin is to blame when you are not there?" The parents replied that he had had similar problems with other teachers. The worker asked, "Does he have these problems with every teacher? If he did, I don't see how the school would have tolerated him for so long." At this point, the parents began to realize that Marvin did get along with some of his teachers and they admitted that maybe he was not fully responsible for what was happening.

After the parents admitted that the problem might not be entirely Marvin's, the worker asked Marvin, "Doesn't your behavior with your teachers make matters worse instead of better?" In this way the family was helped to begin to problem-solve together instead of becoming frustrated, angry, and abusive to each other.

Overt Behavioral Change

This treatment goal requires the worker to intervene directly when abusive parental behavior occurs. For example, a mother who hits her child in frustration might be helped to remove herself from the child's presence when she begins to feel angry. Later in the treatment, the parent might be helped to talk to the child or to use appropriate punishment rather than striking out.

Sometimes the worker allows the abusive behavioral pattern to take place in the session. As an illustration, eight-year-old Yvonne became extremely frustrated whenever she had to do her homework. The mother had two behavioral responses, neither of which was helpful to the child: she either hit Yvonne or did the assignment for her.

The worker requested that Yvonne bring her homework to the

family session. The worker then observed the pattern of interaction between the child and mother and intervened directly. When the child became upset and demanded that the mother help, the worker commented, "Yvonne is giving up and wants you to do the work for her."

When the mother started to do the homework or shout at Yvonne, the worker commented on the mother's frustration and pointed out that she was not letting Yvonne do the work herself. As a result, the mother began to help Yvonne do the work instead of doing it for her. Therefore, the overt behavior that resulted in maltreatment of the child began to change. This case example shows some aspects of problem solving but highlights the worker's focus on changing overt behavior patterns by direct confrontation.

Modification of Systemic Family Processes

In some instance, problems among the other family members, such as a marital conflict that is displaced on the child, can result in child abuse.

Mrs. Martin was angry at her husband for rarely being home, never showing her affection or attention, drinking too much, and not helping in raising their children. However, she feared expressing her anger directly and instead vented her frustration and anger on their youngest child. The worker saw the parents conjointly and encouraged Mrs. Martin to voice her objections and feelings to her husband. It was hoped that as she increasingly stood up to Mr. Martin and the marital relationship improved, she would no longer need to take out her anger on her child.

The goal in treating this family was to modify a maladaptive process within the family system, in this instance the relationship between the marital couple, which was adversely affecting another part of the family system, the parent-child relationship.

There are many different models of family treatment, and no single one has been shown to be the most effective. Each model has a unique focus and employs a set of distinctive techniques. The complex needs and problems of abused and neglected children and their families contraindicate adherence to any one model.

Three different treatment models will be described and then a flexible eclectic approach will be discussed.

Psychoanalytic Family Therapy

Psychoanalytically oriented family therapy relies on detailed, careful history taking (Stierlin 1977; Offer and Vanderstoep 1975; Zinner and Shapiro 1972). Not all family members need be present, and in fact, in some cases work with the total family is considered undesirable. Classical Freudian theory, ego psychology, object relations theory, and self psychology are the theoretical underpinnings for assessment and treatment in the various approaches stemming from this model.

The goal of intensive psychoanalytic family treatment is to help family members to perceive, empathize, and interact with each other as separate and distinct people in the here-and-now, rather than to continue to repeat the past by responding unconsciously as they did within their family of origin. Compared to nonpsychoanalytic family therapists, psychoanalytic therapists are less directive and less focused on overt communication and interactions. Interpretation of patterns, transactions, defenses, resistance, and transference is a major technique.

Structural Family Therapy

Structural family therapy defines family structure as the organized pattern of interaction of family members. It is therefore assumed that dysfunctional family structures maintain problems within a family. The goal of therapy is to change family structure to enable families to solve their problems. This approach does not allow for leisurely history taking or for descriptive accounts. It calls for direct observation of demonstrated behavior. The unique aspect of structural family therapy is the "enactment" within the therapy session. Behavior is changed by actually observing and modifying transactions as they happen, rather than by working with what people say about their relationships. Interventions, interpretations, and strategies are based upon role theory, systems theory, and organizational theory.

Strategic Family Therapy

Strategic family therapy, or problem-solving therapy, brief, or systemic therapy, as it is variously called, is problem-focused. The goal is symptom resolution or solution of the presenting problem, without basically changing the family's structure, developmental level, or enduring patterns of communication and interaction. The focus is on modifying repetitive sequences of behavior that support problems and symptoms. The worker attempts to maximize authority as a means of bringing about change within the family.

A Model for Family Treatment

The model for treating abusive families that we are suggesting draws upon principles and techniques from each of these models and represents a flexible and eclectic approach. In traditional family therapy with nonmaltreating clients, all family members are usually seen without exception. In treatment with abusive families, the worker will often have to be more flexible and begin with the available family members. Assessment, treatment planning, and treatment occur concurrently because the situation is in constant flux. The worker observes and tries to understand family interaction, intervenes if a problem arises, and again observes the interaction following the intervention.

In beginning with the family, the worker should not immediately ask about the abuse but should express interest in getting to know each family member. This engagement technique is referred to as *joining*. The social worker might ask the family about their trip to the agency, in what neighborhood they live, how close are they to the agency, was the trip easy or difficult. Children can be asked what school and grade they are in, what they do for fun, and about their interests or hobbies. Parents can be asked whether they work inside or outside the home. An initial expression of interest in the family and its members is more important in family treatment of child abuse cases than with other cases, because the family is often guarded and expects the worker to be hostile, unfriendly, and judgmental. An approach that immediately probes into the problem can be perceived as assaultive.

Once the practitioner has expressed interest in the family, the next step is to inquire what the family knows or has heard about the agency. The worker should then briefly describe and confirm or clarify the clients' perception of the agency and of treatment. The worker might specifically state that the aim of counseling is to help the entire family with their problems.

The worker is now ready to inquire about the general problems of the family. The counselor observes the family interaction, the roles different people take, who acts as spokesperson to describe the problem, and who might be the family scapegoat. The worker might notice that parents fight whenever the child is mentioned or that parents might use the child as a scapegoat by taking out their anger toward each other on the child. As the worker begins to understand the general problems, he or she begins to plan the steps to be taken to provide some relief. If parents are burdened by reality problems, the worker begins to think of what concrete services might alleviate these problems. If marital discord is displaced onto the child, the worker might consider seeing the parents in marital treatment. In this way, the worker plans treatment goals while assessing the general family problems.

In this family systems perspective, the initial focus is on the presenting problem and how it is perceived by the family members and any other social agencies involved. The worker also determines the ecological fit or misfit between the family and its environment. For example, is there adequate food, shelter, and access to appropriate health care, friends, or extended family? The worker now begins a general inquiry into the problems between the parents and child. The parents are asked about the problems of the child. The child should then be asked about his or her view of the problem. The worker should explicitly state that when children are having problems, parents can be very concerned, upset, and frustrated, and might respond in ways that are not helpful.

Once the social worker has engaged the family and learned something about how the family lives, their reality problems, and their difficulty in getting along with each other, he or she is ready to pinpoint the specific interactions between family members that give rise to abuse.

The worker might ask the parent to describe in detail an event that illustrates the child's problem and the difficulties in disciplining the child. Often, such a specific event has precipitated the family's application to the agency. The family is told that the purpose of this inquiry is to provide the worker with a clear sense of what is going on so that the family can be helped to think through what to do. As the abusive parent describes the "event" the worker should ask specific questions when necessary to get a full picture.

If the parent reports that a child did poorly in school, did not obey, fought with a sibling, or was not interested in school work, the worker should ask what tests or subjects the child failed, what instructions the child did not obey, or what prompted the fight with the sibling. If the parent speaks of screaming at the child, the worker should ask what the parent said. If the parent hit the child, the worker should ask what part of the child's body the parent struck and whether the parent used an open hand or fist. The worker should make no judgment at this point, since the purpose is to get a detailed report of the interaction without prematurely cutting off the discussion.

A case vignette will illustrate how the worker identifies the family interaction that leads to abusive behavior.

Mrs. Rodriquez was a Puerto Rican single parent referred to a family agency after she punched her son and gave him a black eye. As Mrs. Rodriguez discussed what had led to the incident, an interplay occurred that is frequently encountered in family treatment: the mother and Reynaldo began to enact in the session the very hostile kind of interaction that Mrs. Rodriguez had described.

As Mrs. Rodriquez told of her son's terrible report card, he began to roll his eyes. His mother shouted at him for his belligerent attitude and said he'd end up like just another Puerto Rican male cleaning toilets. Reynaldo snapped back that he didn't care. His mother said she didn't care either, he could go find his drug-addicted father and live with him. Reynaldo said that's what he wanted. The mother shouted that both of them could rot in hell.

The worker "blocked" the interaction by observing that although the mother said she didn't care, the fact that she was so angry and concerned suggested she cared very much. In fact the problem seemed to be that she was doing all of the caring for both of them while Reynaldo, who was doing poorly in school, seemed not to care at all. The son now spoke up, saying he was not doing so poorly. The worker asked about his grades and as Mrs. Rodriguez went over each mark, she could see that he actually was not doing so badly and that some teachers had commented that he was trying harder.

In the subsequent sessions, Mrs. Rodriguez spoke about her childhood and differences with her own mother—which contained elements of both adolescent rebellion and cultural conflict. As she talked about the pain and struggle and even maltreatment that she, too, experienced as a child, Reynaldo seemed fascinated and showed great interest. Gradually, a new level of understanding and identification between mother and child began to emerge. Mrs. Rodriguez was more accepting of Reynaldo's need to strive as she once had for identity and independence. Reynaldo reacted to his mother's efforts by trying to be less provocative and more respectful.

Wells (1983) has pointed out that families involved in child abuse often communicate directly through action rather than words. In such instances, the social worker must identify the nonverbal interactions that can lead to the abusive behavior. The worker must permit the destructive interaction to unfold to get a sense of how it starts, but then intervene so that the pattern is not perpetuated. The following case vignette will illustrate how nonverbal interaction gives rise to abusive behavior and how the practitioner can identify the problem and intervene.

Ms. Lewis was referred to a family service agency after beating her eleven-year-old son. She reported that she beat her son Frank because he always beat his younger brother Darnell, aged five. She feared Frank would seriously hurt Darnell.

A general principle in assessing patterns of abuse is to have all family members involved in the abusive interaction participate in the session. In the case of the Lewis family, there were two interrelated problems: Frank's mistreatment of Darnell and Ms. Lewis's mistreatment of Frank. Consequently, the worker saw Ms. Lewis and her children together (there was no father in the home) and detected the following pattern during the sessions. While Ms. Lewis tried to talk to the worker, the boys played a competitive board game. The younger boy, Darnell, would begin to cheat, tease, or act silly to provoke his brother. The older boy would become angry and strike out at Darnell, who then cried out to his mother for help. Ms. Lewis would then shout at Frank.

This pattern was acted out by the family in successive meetings. The worker saw both youngsters alone for three sessions that centered around volley ball play. The pattern of interaction between the siblings was demonstrated even more sharply.

In the third session, the mother was invited to participate. Darnell started to tease Frank, the older boy chased him, and Mrs. Lewis got up to intervene.

The worker asked her to relax and whispered that he would take care of the problem. Frank began to wrestle with Darnell and the younger boy again cried out for his mother. The worker suggested that if she ignored them they would stop. Frank looked over, saw his mother and the worker talking, and let Darnell go. The mother was astonished to see the boys play together for the rest of the session, with Frank actually helping Darnell. The worker suggested that the mother act the same way at home. Three more family sessions were held to reinforce the new family interactional pattern.

In this case, the worker used "role modeling" techniques to help the mother respond in a nonabusive manner to the children. He also established boundaries between the mother and the boys by encouraging her not to interfere.

A common interactional pattern in mild cases of child maltreatment is that of a parent's maltreating the child for not meeting the parent's infantile needs for love, affection, and nurturance. This interactional pattern is often obscured by the parent's complaints about the child's behavior.

The Donovans, an intact family consisting of mother, father, and their eleven-year-old daughter Noreen, were referred to a family service agency because the father had recently started to hit Noreen. They were seen together in family sessions. The parents continually berated Noreen for not obeying, ignoring their criticisms, and "answering back." The parents also complained that Noreen never showed them affection. When the worker explored this, she learned that the father had become enraged and started to hit Noreen after she returned from summer camp. She had angered him by not writing the whole month that she was away. The parents constantly demanded that Noreen show proof of her love. Lately, Noreen was becoming defiant.

An exploration of the parents' histories revealed that they had both been severely neglected and deprived of parenting in early childhood. They tried to give Noreen everything that they lacked but also expected her to shower them with the love and appreciation that they never received from their own parents. It was evident that the parents were unable to differentiate Noreen from themselves and their own needs. Helping them to make this differentiation and find other areas of gratification became the focus of treatment.

Terminating Family Treatment

Once the abusive behavior in a family has stopped, the family must be seen for at least several weeks to consolidate behavioral changes. During this period, the worker offers suggestions to encourage them to continue to practice the new, nonabusive behavioral patterns of interaction that they have learned in the family sessions. For instance, if a family has begun to talk about problems instead of fighting, the worker might suggest that they take some time, every other night, to discuss a problem as they had done in treatment sessions. The family then reports to the worker how they managed the discussion. In this way, the family prepares for termination. In the last family session, the worker might arrange for a "party," especially if there are young children in the family, to celebrate the "graduation" from treatment. Parents might bring in snacks for the children.

In termination with maltreating families, it is important for the worker to plan for a follow-up session with the family, usually six weeks after the ending date. The worker might say, "Let's arrange for an appointment six weeks from now to see how you are getting along." Knowing that they will be returning for the follow-up helps the family to maintain the positive changes that were achieved through counseling. If the worker finds that the family did well in the six-week follow-up, he or she might arrange for a further follow-up in three months.

Selected Techniques and Principles of Family Treatment

Now that the process of family treatment has been described, specific techniques and principles that are particularly useful in family treatment will be defined. These techniques are termed joining, creating boundaries, role modeling, reframing, enactment, verbalization, tasks and directives, and education and guidance.

Joining is a technique that is used to engage the family. When one is seeing a family for the first time, it is helpful for the worker to spend a few minutes speaking individually to each family member about nonthreatening subjects such as where they live or work, or their interests. With this technique, the worker tries to put each family member at ease.

In *creating boundaries*, the worker tries to help parents and children assume appropriate roles. For example, if a child continually interrupts the parent, the worker might say, "You are the parent, why do you allow Johnny to shut you up?" Another example might be a parent's acting seductively toward a child while the other parent is left out. The "left-out" parent might become jealous and react negatively to the child. If the seductive parent and child are seated together and the "left out" parent is seated alone, the worker will create appropriate boundaries by instructing the child and other parent to trade seats so that the parents sit together.

Blocking is a technique the worker uses to set limits on shouting matches between members and to encourage them to talk about their problems more rationally. If family members are continually shouting and interrupting one another, the worker might say, "I know that each of you has important things to say, but we have to take turns or no one will be able to hear what the other is saying." Or the worker might comment, "Yelling and cursing at John doesn't help him understand what you mean. Can you try to talk to him without name calling?" If the family members remain completely unresponsive to these interventions, then family sessions might not be appropriate and they probably need to be seen individually.

In *role modeling,* the worker presents the family with a new model for discipline by not reacting to the child's behavioral problems abusively. For instance, in the family session a child might become destructive with play materials. The worker does not become angry as the parents do, but instructs the child to stop and removes the materials until the child is calmed. If the child is not immediately cooperative, the worker is patient and continues to set limits without becoming angry. In this way, the practitioner demonstrates to the parents a new model for disciplining their children.

In *reframing,* the worker addresses the negative views that family members have toward one another's behavior by pointing out an adaptive or positive side of the behavior. Reframing is an attempt by the worker to alter, modify, or expand the family's view of certain behavior. For instance, a parent might label a child's attempt to do things in his or her own way as "stubborn." The worker might say to the family that the child "has a mind of his own." Or a child who is reacting negatively to a parent's nagging might be helped to see the nagging as an expression of the parent's basic concern for the child.

In *enactment,* the worker tries to help family members act out a problem during the family session (Minuchin and Fishman 1981).

The worker might ask a parent to describe a problem with the child, ask the parent to repeat exactly what is usually said to the child, and then instruct the child to respond as he or she usually does. As mentioned earlier, this technique helps the worker to understand the family's interaction.

Verbalization of feelings is another technique in family treatment. Maltreating families often express their feelings behaviorally instead of verbally. Parents might be frustrated and angry as a result of such reality problems as unemployment, substandard housing, or inadequate income, and may be venting their anger on the child. The worker can encourage the parents to talk about their anger at their many problems instead of taking it out on the child. Parents who physically abuse a child who does not do chores or homework can be encouraged to verbalize their anger instead of hitting the child.

Tasks and directives are additional techniques in family treatment. The family's willingness and ability to perform tasks assigned by the worker help them learn new ways of behaving. If family members do not interact except by fighting, the worker might direct them to carry out some planned activity together that does not result in conflict, such as a family outing or going to the movies.

Education and guidance is another useful technique. For example, parents who leave a young child alone at home should be told that this is harmful and frightening to the child as well as dangerous.

Conclusion

Family treatment is a demanding modality that requires a skilled and experienced practitioner. It is suitable only for mild cases of child maltreatment and is especially useful when specific familial interactions clearly lead to abusive behavior. Therefore, family treatment is not suitable when the abuse is a symptom of severe psychopathology, the consequence of drug or alcohol abuse, or when the maltreatment of the child is severe. Family treatment can be effective even with disorganized, multiproblem families if the treatment remains focused on specific familial interactions.

Family treatment is usually short-term and can be used exclusively, or in conjunction with or in preparation for individual or group therapy. If possible, all members of the immediate family should be drawn into the treatment session.

References

Johnson, H. 1986. Emerging concerns in family therapy. *Social Work* 31:199–206.

Kempe, R., and C. H. Kempe. 1978. *The developing child.* Cambridge: Harvard University Press.

Minuchin, Salvador, and H. Charles Fishman. 1981. *Family therapy techniques.* Cambridge: Harvard University Press.

Mishne, J. M. 1983. *Clinical work with children.* New York: Free Press.

Offer, D., and E. Vanderstoep. 1975. Indications and contraindications for family therapy. In *The adolescent in group and family therapy,* ed. M. Sugar, 145–60. New York: Brunner/Mazel.

Richmond, M. 1922. What is social casework. In *Clinical social work: Theory and practice,* ed. Herbert S. Strean. New York: Free Press, 1978.

Sherman, S. N. 1974. Family therapy. In *Social work treatment: Interlocking theoretical approaches,* ed. Francis J. Turner, 457–92. New York: Free Press.

Stierlin, H. 1977. *Psychoanalysis and family therapy.* New York: Jason Aronson.

Strean, H. S. 1978. *Clinical social work: Theory and practice.* New York: Free Press.

Weitzman, J. 1985. Engaging the severely dysfunctional family in treatment: Basic considerations. *Family Process* 15:473–85.

Wells, Susan J. 1983. A model of therapy with abusive and neglectful families. In *Differential diagnosis and treatment in social work,* 3d ed., ed. Francis J. Turner. London: Free Press.

Zinner, John, and Edward Shapiro. 1972. Projective identification as a mode of perception in families of adolescents. *International Journal of Psychoanalysis* 53: 523–30.

5

Group Treatment

Maxine Lynn, M.S.W.

Introduction

Group treatment is an effective approach in work with maltreatment cases. It has been shown to be effective especially in its ability to provide the opportunity for nurturance and resocialization (Bishop 1983; Barth et al. 1983). No matter how disturbed, most individuals both need and have the capacity to relate to others. Group membership can provide powerful experiences in being accepted and can lead to the development of better communication and other interpersonal skills. Group therapy can provide the atmosphere in which to develop increased empathy for others, new values, attitudes, and behavior, and the control of strong and often unacceptable impulses. Groups are important support networks that diminish individuals' sense of isolation and enhance their ability to take or offer help.

Despite its therapeutic value little has been written about the use of group treatment in maltreatment cases (Shorkey 1979). It may be that the characteristics of this client population, described in earlier chapters, make this modality a difficult one to implement. In addition, the demands on the worker are enormous in a group context and few staff members have been specifically trained in group intervention.

This chapter will define what is meant by group treatment in working with child neglect and abuse cases and will present criteria for its use. It will describe different types of group intervention with children and adults and will discuss and illustrate selected principles and techniques of group intervention. It will comment on some important issues in working with this population and will conclude with a discussion of new directions in group treatment.

Definitions

A group of clients may be defined as an alliance of people who are brought together to work on a common task, to use the group experience for support and mutual aid, for educational purposes, or to effect personality change. Thus group treatment involves different types of groups that have distinctive though sometimes overlapping goals. These range from those that are supportive or educational to those that are more traditionally therapeutic. The nature and tasks of groups also differ depending on whether children, adolescents, or adults are involved.

Criteria

The decision to recommend group treatment should be based on an individualized assessment as described in chapter 2. There are four questions to ask in selecting group intervention:

1. Is some form of group intervention indicated?
2. What type of group is indicated?
3. Should group treatment be the primary or an auxiliary approach?
4. When in the total treatment process should group treatment be introduced?

Group treatment can be the primary modality for dealing with the following difficulties in maltreatment cases:

1. isolation;
2. feelings of hopelessness;
3. mistrust of authority;
4. interpersonal problems;
5. poor socialization skills;
6. poor parenting and child management skills;
7. low self-esteem;
8. poor ego functioning in key areas such as impulse control.

Group treatment can reduce the sense of isolation, stigma, hopelessness, and helplessness that many members of this client population share. It enables the abusing parent to experience a nurturing or corrective positive relationship with the worker and/or other group members. At the same time, the group can also take on an authoritative function, which allows the worker to assume the role of a benign and protective but firm and limit-setting figure. Supportive group experiences are extremely important in helping parents to improve their ego functioning, increase their self-esteem, become more verbally expressive of their feelings, and improve their interpersonal relationships. In addition, groups are useful for the transmission and discussion of factual information regarding child development and child-rearing techniques as well as for developing more realistic expectations of children. In groups in which the participants are children, they too can benefit from peer relationships and can learn to express themselves in nondestructive ways, experience direct nurturance, and get help with various aspects of their ego functioning.

In deciding whether or not to recommend group psychotherapy for adults, it is important to assess a client's motivation and ego strength. Some clinicians have indicated specific criteria by which clients should be excluded from group psychotherapy, including nonpsychological mindedness, secretiveness, acute psychosis, sociopathy, paranoia, brain damage, the use of a great deal of somatization, and lack of motivation for change (Yalom 1985). Obviously, many of the clients involved in abuse and neglect may show these characteristics. However, this does not mean that they should not participate in a group experience.

As opposed to group psychotherapy, more structured, supportive, and educative groups may be helpful in enhancing motivation. If a worker can offer a client a way to meet some personal need through the group, it is possible to help a "resistant" client to use the group modality. For example, an isolated and lonely parent who is resistant to individual counseling may be motivated for group treatment because of the social contact with other parents. A brief clinical vignette will illustrate.

Ms. Rosen was referred to a social agency for treatment by the child protective agency because she was mildly abusing her two- and four-year-old children. In her interview with the intake worker, she argued that she did not need individual counseling.

Ms. Rosen: I do not have any problems except for being imprisoned all winter in the house with these children. There is no place for me to go with them. I don't know any other parents and it is too cold to sit in the park all day. I sit in the house all day and these children drive me crazy. How will counseling change that?

Intake worker: It sounds as if you need some contact with other parents— some adult companionship. Do you know that we have a group for parents in your situation?

Ms. Rosen: Now that sounds interesting.

Many clients will be fearful of exposure in groups, overstimulated by some group experiences, and may lack the impulse control to tolerate the stirring up of intense feelings. But the worker can effectively structure the group to deal specifically with these issues and may be helpful in enabling the client to participate in group experiences.

A more selective and useful list of exclusion criteria for adults would include:

1. extreme paranoia;
2. poor impulse control to a degree that violent acts could occur in group;
3. an immature ego structure that prevents ability to hear other members; and
4. excessive demands for the worker's total attention.

Substance abusers present a particular set of problems (see chapter 8) and should be referred into specific groups for that difficulty. In the most serious situations of child abuse or neglect, group treatment cannot be the only modality but needs to be combined with case management and individual or family treatment. Zalba excluded from groups parents who exhibit uncontrollable physical abuse. He recommended it as a primary modality for parents with controllable abuse and for impulsive but adequate parents with either marital or identity/role conflicts (Zalba 1967).

With respect to recommending children for group treatment, there are other considerations. While the young preschool child is too self-centered for group involvement to any degree (Hartford 1971), neglected and abused latency-age children can benefit from groups. Many have gaps in language development, impulse control problems, and difficulty handling separation from a parent (Bishop 1983). The specialized play group allows these children to receive nurturance and to improve their socialization and cognitive skills. Most of these children have particular problems with aggression and self-esteem. They feel isolated and alienated from peers, and they distrust adults. Group intervention can help the child deal with self-esteem, poor peer relationships, distrust of others, and avoidance of closeness. The group can give the child the opportunity to learn to belong and share. It can be an ideal corrective emotional experience and can supply missing nurturance and care.

Like adults, there are some children who should be excluded from groups. These include 1. children who have exhibited psychotic behavior, i.e., children who have retreated totally into fantasy; 2. children who are extremely aggressive; and 3. children with no social skills. These children need a specialized group experience, residential treatment, or a period of individual treatment.

Variations of Group Treatment

In considering the usefulness of group intervention for a particular client, it is important to review the many different types of groups for children and adults. These include: activity groups, psychotherapy groups, parent education and skills groups, behavior modification groups, support and mutual aid groups, self-help groups, and group psychotherapy. These groups have both distinctive and overlapping foci and techniques.

With special and complex needs, maltreated children and their parents often require a blend of different approaches. To work best with this population, the group worker must use different techniques selectively depending on the changing goals of the group and the needs and problems of the members. The main types of group treatment are described below.

Groups for Children and Adolescents

Activity groups are very important in work with children and preadolescents. Since children symbolize through play and express themselves through action, activity is viewed as therapeutic. The activity group for preadolescents blends the use of program and play to help the children improve their ego functioning and interpersonal skills, to express themselves, and to develop effective limits. Abused and neglected children will tend to bring into the group interaction the familial patterns of abuse. A brief clinical vignette will illustrate.

Brian, a ten-year-old group member, came from a family in which he was physically abused by his mother. It seemed that within the family, Brian could get his mother's attention only by acting silly or provocative. She responded to his negative behavior by hitting him. She then felt bad and would make up to him, giving Brian attention for a limited period. Brian brought this negative way of gaining attention into the group. He would tease and provoke the others until someone became angry. He would then act remorseful and sullen until the other boy made up with him. (Appropriate worker intervention in response to similar behavior will be discussed later.)

Activity groups are generally aimed at increasing attention span, increasing cooperation, building cohesiveness, and task mastery. In the case of abused children, activity groups serve the additional function of permitting the youngsters to develop new patterns of interaction other than the abusive interaction.

The process of the group is more important than the activity itself. The children generally plan a snack time and will celebrate birthdays and holidays. In planning and engaging in such activities, the youngsters will often spontaneously discuss how such occasions are celebrated at home and the kind of disappointments, frustrations, and pleasures they experience. For instance, in one such group the children became quite messy and disorderly during snack time. One boy began to discuss how he would be "killed" at home if he ever acted this way. His statement opened up a spontaneous discussion of how the boys feared their parents and also what behavior on their part gave rise to their parents' rage.

As the child gets older, less activity is needed. The abused preadolescent has often had to develop coping mechanisms that place the child in an adult role. The fluctuations of childish and precocious behavior are more severe, requiring the worker to be more flexible and tolerant but also to intervene when there is group destructive behavior. Children who are severly abused and neglected often engage in behavior that leaves them quite vulnerable. The less they are protected in the family, the less likely it is that they will protect themselves. If a group of neglected or abused children is formed, they will inevitably engage in some form of group testing to learn if the group leader will behave as the parents by either abusing them in retaliation or by not caring and not protecting them.

Principles of Intervention When the Group Tests the Leader

If the group members begin to misbehave to test the leader, the worker should not respond in an abusive or retaliatory manner as the abusive parents do. Instead, the worker should assume an overt protective function by saying, "I will not allow anyone in the group to hurt himself or one another or the property in the room. My job is to protect the group and each one of you."

It will be noted that the worker brings herself into the intervention by saying, "I will not allow you to hurt yourselves," as opposed to simply saying, "You are not allowed to hurt yourselves . . ." In this way, the worker's protective stance is emphasized and drawn to the attention of the children. The following vignette will illustrate the group process of testing the leader.

A group of neglected and abused youngsters who were seen in a mental health clinic housed in a community center clandestinely planned a "trip" to the roof of the building after the group session. They were spotted on the roof by passers-by and the clinic was informed. In the next group session, the group leader brought up how the group was seen on the roof and wandering through the community center. The group leader then remained quiet for a time to see how the group would respond. One group member cautioned the others that they better not get in trouble again or the group leader might kill them. They discussed how the group leader might be angry because he could be "fired" for their behavior. Another boy imagined what might happen to the group leader if one of them were to have fallen off the roof. Some of the boys came from families where they could literally do whatever they wanted up to the point at which their behavior in the community either brought attention to the parents or began to inconvenience the parents. At this point, the parents would suddenly take notice and severely beat the children, not out of concern for the children but rather out of concern for themselves.

The group leader waited until the pattern of interaction became clear and then intervened, based upon an understanding of what familial patterns the boys enacted in the group. The leader stated in the same session that the boys should never go on the roof again, not because the leader would get fired or hurt in some way, but rather because one of them could be hurt. The leader spoke to them about how someone could fall off a roof unintentionally and that the group itself, and the leader, needed to protect each member. The leader made certain in the boys' presence that the maintenance crew found a way to bar the roof from access, thereby indicating concern for their safety. In sessions that followed, the boys began to discuss how they could do anything they wanted at home—stay out late, get into all sorts of trouble—and some of the boys began to speak up about how dangerous such behavior could be.

Gradually, the group began to develop an ideal of self-concern and protection. If one of the boys began to handle a tool or behave in a manner dangerous to himself, the other members would intervene even before the therapist, telling the at-risk member that he should take care of himself. The term "take care of yourself" became the motif of the group.

This clinical vignette demonstrates how the group leader intervenes by not acting in the same way as the parent—by becoming either abusive or neglectful—but instead demonstrates concern and protection and thus helps to change the boys' interaction.

There have been few groups designed specifically for physically abused or neglected adolescents. The abused adolescent may sometimes appear in group psychotherapy for mixed problems. These youngsters will sometimes run away and become involved in delinquent activities as a result of the abuse. They may be apprehended for this behavior and remanded to shelters. These abused adolescents can benefit from groups specifically designed for problems of abuse as well as from mixed groups.

In the group treatment of adolescents, it is important that the group leader promote group members' support of one another, to combat the usual tendency of abused children to blame themselves for their parents' abuse. When a child assumes blame for the abuse, the worker says, "I notice that you always blame yourself and believe it is your fault that your parent beat or criticized you. You never think that maybe your parents had some problems that you suffered for." The worker then tries to promote the other adolescents to support the abused member by asking, "Do you think Mary is as bad as Mary says she is? What do you think about the problem between Mary and her parents?" The following clinical vignette will illustrate how the group leader continues to encourage other group members to support an abused youngster.

Mary was a sixteen-year-old girl in a mixed adolescent group of this type. Her mother often both verbally and physically abused her and made her feel inadequate, that she could not do anything right. In the group, she would often criticize herself in much the same manner that her mother put her down. The group took issue with Mary's low opinion of herself and wondered where she ever developed such a poor self-image. At this point, Mary began to tell the group of incidents at home in which she was abused. The group provided her with much support by showing her that her emotionally disturbed mother often responded too strongly to minor infractions. Mary would tell the group of something she had done, such as receiving a "B" instead of an "A" on a test, and how her mother called her retarded and did not speak to her for days, or how Mary gained four pounds and her mother called her a fat slob. The group responded that her mother was crazy, that a "B" did not make Mary retarded, and that additional pounds did not make her a fat slob. Through the group's support, Mary became less depressed and self-blaming and better able to stand up to her mother. The group leader intervened simply by asking the group what it thought when Mary reported that she deserved to die because her mother said she was retarded for receiving a "B". This intervention set in motion the group's support of Mary.

Groups for Adults

Groups for adults can focus on parent education and/or parenting skills, mutual aid or support, behavioral modification, or insight and group interaction.

It is often stated that one can go to school to learn about almost anything, including how to drive a car, but where and how does one learn to be a parent? The lack of this kind of education and its consequences are most clear in abusive and neglectful parents who have had poor or nonexistent role models. Therefore, groups that aim at improving parenting skills for abusive parents often focus upon improving verbal communication as an alternative to physical discipline and on enhancing impulse control and social skills. Parents are taught to discipline effectively through reasonable punishments, setting of limits, and learning about the particular needs of their children. Parents are also taught not to be overly giving in such a way that their resentment builds up when the child does not return or appreciate their self-sacrifice. Parents are also taught to give approval, affection, and attention to their children, as will be shown in later vignettes.

Another important aspect of treatment in adult groups is mutual aid. Such mutual aid involves "an alliance of individuals who need each other in varying degrees to work on common problems" (Schwartz 1974, 218). Gitterman and Shulman (1986, 362) defined the mutual aid system in the group as a system in which "people share relevant concerns and ideas and begin to experience others in the same 'boat' moving through the rocky waters of life. . . . As they confide, share and move into taboo areas, they feel less singled out, their concerns/ problems become less unique, less unusual and often less pathological. By its very nature the group mutual aid system universalizes peoples' problems, reducing isolation and stigma. . . . This unleashes a group's inherent potential for multiplicity of helping relationships, with all members invested and participating in the helping process."

A mutual aid-oriented group can be especially helpful to mildly or potentially abusive parents. A clinical vignette will illustrate.

Mrs. Barnes joined a mothers' support group. She felt like an unnatural mother to her two-year-old child because she did not always feel love for the infant, sometimes wished to be rid of her, felt trapped in caring for her, and sometimes had disturbing thoughts about throwing the baby out of the window. Mrs. Barnes was the type of person who always had to present a good, dutiful, positive outlook to other people. She never revealed negative thoughts to anyone. To the world she acted the role of the dutiful, enthusiastic mother, while her negative feelings were pent up inside of her and threatened to explode. In the group, she at first presented only enthusiasm and love of motherhood. However, as she heard other mothers complain and sometimes describe their children in less than glowing terms, Mrs. Barnes felt greatly relieved and gradually shared her own negative feelings. She found that as she could tell the group of her wish sometimes to throw her infant out of the window—a thought she'd never act upon—she felt increasingly less resentful and better able to take care of her baby.

It should be added, however, that a group that is predominantly mutual aid or self-help is most suitable for parents who would not actually physically harm the child and have no history of psychiatric disturbances, impulse control problems, or serious emotional disturbance. Parents who might physically harm a child usually need individual treatment, sometimes in combination with group treatment.

Another form of group treatment, group psychotherapy, is often an effective modality for mildly abusive parents who have some capacity for self-awareness. Group therapy tries to resolve problems related to earlier developmental phases and to promote better ego functioning and self-esteem. The psychotherapy group can provide parents with an identification with the group as a whole as well as with the members or the leader. Scheidlinger noted that for the individual the group can be a symbolic representation of a nurturing mother (Scheidlinger 1982). He further stated that in group treatment of people with deprived backgrounds, ego disturbances, and identity "diffusion," the perception of the group in a supportive and benign way can be most important for treatment (Scheidlinger 1982). Many abusive parents come from such deprived backgrounds and can gain some benefit from the mutual identification, support, and nurturance of the group.

Selected Group Treatment Principles and Techniques with Maltreated Children

Preparatory Phase: How to Begin

Let us first explore the way in which the group should be structured. The size of the group should be between six and eight members. This is large enough to allow for interaction, while also small enough to enable individual needs to be met. The children should be the same gender and about the same age, since latency-age children generally relate well to youngsters of their own gender. Adolescent groups can include both genders. Children need a spacious room, and the items that the children play with should be visible and accessible. The worker might set out arts and crafts material, clay, games, drawing materials, and construction items. This selection of play materials allows children to play individually or cooperatively. The play material should be for making or building things, or it should allow for the expression of family conflicts. Family puppet sets can be used expressively.

The worker establishes initial contact by introducing himself or herself, and then asks group members to introduce themselves and encourages them to get to know one another. The worker can facilitate this by asking each of the children about their schools, grades, and neighborhoods. The children usually know something about one another's schools or know someone attending another child's school, and they begin talking to one another. The worker should then tell the children that the purpose of the group is to help with problems and that the children may play and make whatever they like. The worker announces the day and time that the group will regularly meet and that there will be a snack (usually milk and cookies) at the midpoint of every session. The snack period provides the group with a natural opportunity to begin to talk.

After completing this introduction in the group, the worker steps back and allows the children to explore the room and the play materials and to choose what they wish to do. If some children appear lost and in need of direction, the worker should approach them individually and ask if they need help. With children who still cannot make a choice the worker should mention a few possibilities but still encourage them to choose for themselves. In this way, the worker begins to encourage self-initiative.

Principles of Intervention in Activity Group Therapy with Maltreated Children

So far, the beginning of the group as described above would be typical of any child activity group. However, abused and neglected children often present some special problems even in the very beginning. Children who are abused or neglected often dislike themselves and what they make. It is very difficult for children to like or value themselves and what they produce when they have been rejected, mistreated, and unprotected. The result may be that the children will become destructive toward the play material. A maltreated child often communicates through action and behavior rather than verbally. Therefore, the worker should intervene by actions directed toward the child's behavior and not by verbally oriented insight techniques. The following clinical vignette will illustrate how the leader acts to intervene.

Roger, a ten-year-old abused boy, would begin to work on arts and crafts but quickly become disgusted and give up. In frustration, he became destructive toward the material he was working with. A special problem of intervention arises here. Abused and neglected children are often made to feel inadequate and weak in their families if they ask for help. Therefore, if the worker makes too great a show of trying to help, the child might feel humiliated and inadequate in the presence of the other group members. The child imagines that the group "thinks" just like his or her family. Since the other children have also been abused and neglected, this might well be true. If the worker makes a demonstration of the child's need for help, the group will often begin to tease and scapegoat the youngster. The worker approached Roger, told him destruction of play materials was not allowed, and asked him if he needed help. Roger replied, "No."

The worker immediately backed off but waited for Roger to give up on the next project he had started. Before Roger could begin to destroy it, the worker approached and asked him if the worker could keep the unfinished project. Roger nodded. At the beginning of the next session, the worker showed Roger that he had preserved and valued Roger's unfinished project. Henceforth, whenever Roger gave up on a project, the worker approached and asked if he could save it. At the beginning of sessions, Roger began to ask the worker if he had preserved the latest unfinished project. The worker showed him it. Roger began to offer the worker his unfinished projects. One day, Roger called the therapist over and asked for his help in completing a project.

This clinical vignette illustrates a specific principle of intervention with abused children. The worker intervened through action by saving Roger's productions instead of through interpreting or discussing with Roger his feelings of inadequacy and frustration. Abusive families often communicate through actions and not through words. It would be premature and possibly destructive for the therapist to attempt to have such children share or verbalize feelings in this initial phase of treatment. The therapist shows empathy by first addressing the actions of the child and by showing in the worker's own actions an understanding of the child's actions. By saving the child's productions, the worker communicated that he valued the child. By not offering help too aggressively, the worker communicated that he understood that needing help was a sign of weakness and inadequacy for the child.

Principles of Intervention in the Middle Phase of Treatment

In the middle phase of treatment in activity groups, children increasingly bring into the group the familial patterns of abusive interaction. The group becomes a "substitute family" for each child. The children recreate the familial interaction in the group through their behavior and actions; the worker intervenes by addressing the pattern of action. This intervention enables the youngsters to begin to discuss their feelings and their family life. The following brief vignette illustrates this middle phase of treatment.

Anthony, an abused youngster who was ten years old, always seemed to want whatever another boy had. If another boy painted, Anthony wanted to use the very paints the boy was working with. When Anthony spotted a boy making crafts, Anthony wanted to use those materials. At snack time, Anthony would clandestinely snatch another boy's cookies when he wasn't looking. The other children began to call Anthony a "grabber" and began to hit him when he approached.

The worker intervened by saying, "Anthony, you always want whatever the other boy has." As Anthony would approach another youngster to "grab," the worker would ask, "Anthony, do you again want what Jimmy has?" Anthony would giggle and back off. The other children stopped hitting at Anthony as he approached and instead teased, "Do you want what I have again, Anthony?" The boys as a group now no longer permitted Anthony to "grab" from any one boy. During snack, one boy commented to Anthony, "You would want my milk even if it were sour."

Anthony saw his point and began to talk to the other boys about how everyone in his family behaved this same way. He reported that if he watched TV, his father or older siblings would walk in and change the channel if they wished to see something else. If Anthony protested, he was hit. At mealtime, everyone grabbed for food and the older siblings always took the most. One of the boys said Anthony probably behaved the same way and Anthony laughed and said he always took whatever his younger siblings had and hit them if they protested.

The group discussion led to what was earlier termed the mutual aid process. In the next meeting, one of the boys said he was not too hungry and offered Anthony a cookie. Another boy offered to share his paints with Anthony. As the group became more "giving," Anthony became less "grabbing." In school, teachers reported that Anthony's behavior dramatically improved as he stopped fighting with peers, the original problem for which he was referred to the group.

The above vignette demonstrates how the worker can intervene to promote the mutual aid process.

Children even as young as six can be helpful to each other. In children's groups, one child will help another with homework, one child will save part of a lunch for another child. However, in groups of neglected and abused children, the children may be so deprived that they will not always share with one another but may instead tend to hold on to their own possessions and try to take someone else's away. The group's initial interaction might be to abuse and reject one another and to expect abuse, rejecting, and grabbing from one another. The worker's alertness and identification of the patterns of behavioral interaction as demonstrated above can help the group arrive at a mutual aid process.

As the children begin to trust one another and lessen their mutually abusive or defensive interaction, they begin to reveal to one another their experiences of being abused in the family. They are often angry and feel helpless. Some of the stories may be exaggerated to catch everyone's attention. The worker will have to deal with the horrific stories that the children present, and not become caught in a pervading helpless feeling; this can be done by engaging members in problem solving. However, children have considerable limitations in their ability to change the abusive interactions in the family. Even if the child contributes toward the abusive interaction by provocative behavior, there is definitely no guarantee that the abuse will cease because the child changes his or her behavior or asserts himself or herself with the family. Therefore, the problem-solving efforts with the children have severe limitations, and it is absolutely necessary that the abusive parents also receive help or that the child be protected by the responsible authorities. Actually, it is with the parents that problem-solving efforts most urgently need to be made.

Ending Phase

The ending phase may occur two ways. One child may leave the group, or the entire group may end. This usually depends on whether the group is time-limited and closed or open-ended and long-term. During the ending phase of time-limited groups the worker needs to help the children separate from the individual identification they each have with the leader and the group. In long-term groups the worker must assess when a child has gone as far as possible in the group and is ready to move on. A child may grow out of a group and need a different kind of experience. In both instances the child must mourn the loss of the group. For example, the worker might plan for a special party to acknowledge a child's last group session. The leader might then turn to the child who is terminating and ask, "Johnny, why don't you say something about what the group has been like today and what you are feeling about leaving it?" The worker might further help Johnny to discuss termination by adding, "Remember the day you started the group? Let's look at all that's happened since then." The leader should also ask the other group members how they feel about Johnny's leaving and whether they feel sad about it.

It also is important for the worker to help the children to recognize that there are other supportive adults in their lives to whom they can turn—guidance counselors, teachers, librarians—and other group opportunities—scouts, after-school programs, church groups. In instances where the worker is leaving or ending the group, it is especially important for the worker to take responsibility for this action and to clarify and work through the reasons for it so that the children will not blame themselves.

During the termination phase of the group or when one child is leaving there are several other important interventions. The worker should:

1. explore the children's feelings about previous endings and losses, being especially sensitive to their feelings of abandonment and blame;
2. help the child or children to identify, reach out to, or maintain relationships with other supportive adults;
3. help group members to review their progress and what the group has meant to them;
4. make appropriate referrals.

Selected Group Treatment Principles and Techniques with Adults

Preparatory Phase: How to Begin

As with children's groups, groups for abusive parents should comprise six to eight members in order to allow for interaction and individualized attention. There should be some balance in membership. Parents who are not conflicted and self-righteous in their methods of discipline need to be mixed with parents who consider their methods of discipline a problem. The worker may have individual meetings with potential members to assess the severity of the abuse and to prepare them for the group. Parents with serious emotional problems will need to be seen in individual treatment exclusively or in conjunction with a group.

Other distinctive issues in working with adults involve the need for clarification of issues related to confidentiality and mandatory reporting if there are instances of abuse or neglect and the need to arrange child care and transportation options to ensure attendance.

Principles of Intervention in Group Treatment with Maltreating Parents

In the first meeting, the group leader asks the members to introduce themselves and to present some identifying information, such as where they live, whether they work in or out of the home or attend school or take part in other activities, how old and in what grade their children are. The group leader then provides a brief orientation to the agency and its services. The leader shows empathy by saying, "Parenting can be quite difficult and we will work toward the group members' helping one another both as parents and persons." The group leader explains that his or her function is to promote that process. The leader should then ask group members if they have any further questions. In the first meeting the leader focuses on helping the members get to know one another. Once this orientation is complete, the leader asks the members to describe their difficulties with their children and how they have attempted to handle these situations. The leader waits for members to speak rather than ordering them to do so. Through this action, the leader conveys to members that they are expected to speak but at their own pace.

In most treatment groups, the worker reinforces interactions among members by helping them to express and understand their feelings. In work with abusive parents, prematurely focusing on feelings can be dangerous and threatening for some members. Abusive parents tend to express feelings through action; rage is often the predominant feeling. Clients with poor impulse control will often be overwhelmed by ventilation of feelings. It would be unrealistic for the group leader to expect abusive parents to express feelings initially. The worker should begin by asking parents to describe the events, situations, and actions that illustrate the problems with their children. Abusive parents might feel more comfortable discussing events rather than feelings. The worker might initiate the discussion of actual events as follows:

> Ms. Woods (a group member): Della is getting arrogant again. I don't know who that child thinks she is. If she keeps this up, she'll get a slap in the face. I can't stand her attitude.
>
> Worker: Can you describe an incident, from the beginning, where she became arrogant? Why don't you give us an example describing what she actually said and did and how you responded so we can try to help.

In the beginning phase, the worker generally intervenes by attempting to have other group members help the client experiencing problems.

For example, when one of the parents describes a problem with a child, the leader can ask the other members, "What do you think about the problem?" Later, when the parents are at ease with group interaction, the worker might ask the other members, "How do you think Ms. Jones dealt with her child?" and still later, "Do any of you have ideas about how Ms. Jones might deal more effectively with her child?" The worker fosters group intervention to facilitate interaction and because members are often at first less defensive and more open to comments made by other parents in the same situation than by the group leader. Abusive parents will tend to be especially mistrustful of the authority of the leader, so that interventions that promote the group to respond are especially useful. In the initial phase, group members tend to be cautious with one another, so the response is usually not overly confrontive. A clinical case example will illustrate.

> Mrs. McDonald reported week after week how badly her son behaved. The group empathized with what a handful he was. One week, Mrs. McDonald reported that her son was not doing his math assignments but watching television instead, so she threw the television out and hit him. She said that she'd throw him out next. The leader intervened by asking the group what they thought of Mrs. McDonald's problem. Another member, Mrs. Ortiz, who had similar problems and attitudes with her own child, was able to see Mrs. McDonald's problem with much greater objectivity than she could see her own. She replied that she felt throwing out the television and hitting her son was a bit too much. She began to suggest other means by which Mrs. McDonald might have dealt with her child. Mrs. McDonald insisted that she had tried to no avail whatever Mrs. Ortiz suggested. She complained that her son was impossible. This session saw no agreement or resolution for the problem. But in the next session, Mrs. McDonald said she had thought over

what Mrs. Ortiz said, that maybe she did tend to go too far and that she was trying to get her child to study by encouragement and praise.

The intervention described above requires a degree of patience on the part of the leader. The first couple of times the worker asks the group what it thinks about a parent's problem, the group might agree with the parent or not respond. However, it is in the nature of a group situation that as the members become comfortable they will tend to speak out more. One of the advantages of the group is that parents can respond much more objectively to problems quite similar to their own when another member suffers from them. Also, the natural competitiveness among members for the leader's attention will result in their differing with one another. In some instances, the worker might encourage the group to respond and the group might begin to attack the member. In such instances, it will be necessary for the leader to support the attacked member while not invalidating the truth in the criticisms.

Mrs. Siegel discussed how her daughter was torturing the family cat. Mrs. Siegel slapped her around for this. The worker asked the group what they thought and if they could be of help to Mrs. Siegel. One member said the daughter tortured the cat because Mrs. Siegel always slapped her around. Another member said that the daughter would probably like to torture Mrs. Siegel but was afraid to so she tortured the cat instead. Mrs. Siegel began to cry and acknowledged that she did have a problem controlling her temper with her daughter and felt terrible about it. Another member who never seemed to like Mrs. Siegel now angrily joined in and began listing everything that she did not like about Mrs. Siegel that needed changing. Another member allied with the attacker added further complaints that removed the subject far from the original issue of abuse. The worker now intervened to support Mrs. Siegel by saying, "The group will not help Mrs. Siegel by verbally slapping her around any more than Mrs. Siegel helped her daughter by physically slapping her around."

Principles of Intervention in the Middle Phase

The middle phase of group treatment is characterized by parents' talking more openly about their abusive problems, how they were sometimes abused themselves as children, and by the parents' bringing patterns of abusive familial interaction into the group. In the middle phase, the group should increasingly trust and perceive the worker as a helper and not only as an authoritative figure. The principles of intervention during this phase involve the worker's intervening directly with a client's abusive behavior, especially if the group avoids doing so. The following clinical vignette will illustrate this kind of intervention.

A group of abusive fathers was in the middle phase of treatment. Mr. Lewis recently married a woman with a twelve-year-old son. Mr. Lewis was physically abusive to the boy even though the child was well-behaved. Mr. Lewis said he could not stand how the boy, John, was sensitive, awkward, and clung to his mother's apron strings. Mr. Lewis was referred by Special Services for Children after his wife reported him for beating the youngster with a belt. In the initial phase of the group, Mr. Lewis complained that his stepson was a wimp and unmanly but added that he was no longer hitting him because his wife would report him. However, Mr. Lewis reported instances of verbally abusing and threatening the boy and the group did not confront him. The group leader encouraged the group to respond and try to help Mr. Lewis, but the group seemed afraid of this angry, self-righteous client. In the middle phase, when Mr. Lewis had developed a sense of the leader's concern, the worker intervened by saying to Mr. Lewis, "Your son's behavior did not seem to warrant the anger and name calling that you inflicted." Once the worker intervened, the group joined in and members pointed out that Mr. Lewis' only complaints about his son were that he took a nap after school sometimes, that he cried when Mr. Lewis abused him, and that he sometimes talked to his mother about what bothered him. Other group members said that they wished their children were as well-behaved as John and wondered why Mr. Lewis disliked him. Such interventions resulted in Mr. Lewis recalling that he had tortured a younger brother in the same way because their mother doted on him. Mr. Lewis could now see that he was jealous of his son's relationship to his mother.

Another principle of intervention in the middle phase involves the leader's facilitating problem-solving activity among the group members. During the middle phase, parents can be helped to problem solve.

Mrs. Marks could not say no to her son, but became resentful that the son never stopped demanding and did whatever he wished. She finally became enraged and beat him. The leader encouraged the group to help by asking, "Do any of you want to offer any help to Mrs. Marks?", and they discussed with her how she could begin to say no to her youngster before the interaction got out of hand. When she reported setting limits on his unreasonable demands, the group offered her praise.

Mrs. Jackson increasingly realized that she had a low threshold of tolerance for her daughter Melinda's ordinary needs for attention. The group helped her figure out how much attention she could tolerate giving to her child and how much time she needed for herself. The group also helped her to go for a walk to blow off steam instead of striking her daughter. The leader facilitated these interventions by asking the group to try to help her.

In such instances, the worker attempts to balance the group's providing help with the individual members' thinking for themselves. When the group becomes too zealous about giving advice and the client appears overwhelmed, the worker might say, "Maybe Mr. Jones needs to think about this for himself and see what is right for him. What works for the others might not work for Mr. Jones." If an individual member rejects help from others and always dismisses the others' suggestions, the worker might point out how the client finds it difficult to accept or take in help and feels he or she must think of everything independently even if it isn't working out well. The worker then might ask what the client fears in asking for help.

In the middle phase, the clients sometimes bring into the group the familial patterns of abusive interaction. The principle of intervention is for the leader to identify that interaction explicitly.

In the group of fathers, Mr. Pittman reported incidents of his sons' delinquent behavior in such a way that clearly indicated that he enjoyed their acting out and encouraged their delinquency. However, when they landed in some type of trouble that embarrassed the family, he would beat them. In the group, Mr. Pittman was encouraging another father to beat the system by fraud. The worker intervened and identified the familial pattern of interaction recapitulated in the group by commenting that Mr. Pittman wanted to turn the other client into a "delinquent." The use of the term delinquent encouraged another father to remark that Mr. Pittman always complained his sons were delinquents. In the next few weeks, Mr. Pittman began to notice how he encouraged his sons to be delinquents in the same way, then became enraged and abusive when they were caught. Mr. Pittman then told the father he had tried to corrupt that if the other had taken his advice, and then was caught, Mr. Pittman would have been the first to say how stupid the other was.

Ending Phase

Endings occur because the group is no longer going to meet, or the worker departs prematurely, or some member leaves the group. In all instances, issues around separation and loss need to be focused on. This can be very painful for clients who have been abandoned and/or rejected repeatedly and who often have felt blamed. Dealing with endings is particularly important in maltreatment cases in order to help members consolidate the gains they have made and to prevent a regression to past more maladaptive modes of dealing with problems and impulses.

In dealing with endings, the worker should:

1. stress the interconnections among group members;
2. focus on what they have accomplished;
3. help group members identify, connect with, and maintain outside supportive relationships;
4. focus on the subjective meaning the ending has for each group member, including its stirring up of past issues;
5. stress not only the issue of loss but also the chance for new beginnings.

Special Issues

Maltreatment cases generate many unresolved feelings and reactions in the worker that are intensified in group treatment. The worker has to deal with tremendous complexity in each situation. In order to reduce the demands, agencies need to be supportive and the worker needs to mobilize the group properties that diffuse its intense demands quickly. The level of comfort with painful issues stemming from the worker's own past is an important factor in being able to be attuned to group members. It may be highly beneficial to have several coleaders or adjunct staff at each session. This helps the workers deal with the intensity and demands of the group experience. At the same time, it tends to help the members feel safer and increases their sense of being nurtured.

Group formation becomes a difficult task from the outset. One reason is the scattering of cases to many agencies and workers in order not to burden any specific one. Even when attendance is mandated by the court and clients live within a reasonable distance of the agency, considerable outreach may be necessary to ensure members' continuance in the group.

Group work usually is based on values of democratic participation, confidentiality, and self-determination of members. With this population, however, confidentiality has to be modified since certain behaviors must be reported. This affects the trust needed to build a cohesive environment. Likewise, group members may be required to attend. Success requires regular, ongoing attendance. The worker will need constantly to address dropout rates, reach out to ensure compliance, and deal with lateness. Even with authoritative motivation for attendance, members can nevertheless use groups effectively (Bellucci 1972).

Group members need to feel secure and nurtured by the group as well as by the leader. Members may be so needy that they cannot give to others. This may require the worker to give direct expressions of nurturance and/or to model this behavior. Even in psychotherapy groups, it may be necessary to arrange transportation, provide child care, and give coffee or snacks. Likewise, while striving for shared and peer leadership, the worker may have to be more active, offer a more structured environment, and take control of the process, at least in its initial phases.

Group treatment passes through a sequence of developmental stages, with members expressing more dependency needs initially and moving through conflict resolution and stages in which intimacy becomes the major dynamic. Groups specific for this population (either abusers or abused) tend to move at a much slower rate. Parents who abuse usually do not trust other adults, especially professional workers. The use of a group allows the member to reduce negative reactions to the worker, and members can develop positive feelings toward each other and the group while remaining distant from the worker. The member can feel less threatened in a group. Another modification may be the use of group members as active supports to each other between sessions. In contrast to traditional ways of doing group psychotherapy, one may encourage exchange of phone numbers between members. Members may also benefit from organized activity such as planned trips, outings, and guest speakers to address special interests of the members.

Extensions and New Developments

The group modality is an excellent preventive tool for high-risk groups and can provide supportive parenting education. It is also useful for identification of abuse and neglect cases in children's groups, particularly in latency adjustment groups and rap groups. Often the child who is abused is not doing well in school and is secretive and unable to relate with peers. The child's behavior in the group can be a signal for what is happening in the home.

Child abuse situations often involve numerous social agencies and professionals in managing the case. It would probably be more efficient to bring the team that is dealing with the situation together with a coordinator-leader. This use of group techniques would lead to a comprehensive treatment plan and reduce some of the demands on individual agencies and workers. The frustrations would lessen and team members could feel satisfaction from working in a mutual aid system.

Practitioners working with child abuse cases face a great deal of stress that can lead to burnout. Agencies report considerable turnover in staff who deal with these situations. The use of leaderless support groups could provide the staff with the nurturing self-care that they need. The workers need a good support system. The use of this modality by child protection workers was reported by Bandoli (1977).

A new development in the field has been the placement of agency personnel in local schools and some churches, which makes them visible to the community. Children need to be taught in school how and when to go for help. A self-referral system can be implemented for children. This can lead to a drop-in center for children where open-ended groups can be run at selected times on-site in public schools. Similarly, families may need help becoming familiar with their local family agency or mental health center, so that when they feel stress they know where to turn.

References

Bandoli, L. 1977. Leaderless support groups in child protective services. *Social Work* 22 (March): 150–51.

Barth, R., et al. 1983. Self-control training with maltreating parents. *Child Welfare* 62 (4): 313–25.

Bellucci, M. 1972. Group treatment of mothers in child protection cases. *Child Welfare* 2 (2): 110–16.

Bishop, E. 1983. Mother-toddler group therapy. In *Child abuse and neglect: A guide with case studies for treating the child and family,* ed. N. Ebeling and D. Hill, 183–205. Littleton, Mass.: PSG Inc.

Gitterman, A., and L. Shulman, eds. 1986. *Mutual aid groups and the life cycle.* Itasca, Ill.: F. E. Peacock Publishers.

Hartford, M. 1971. *Groups in social work, applications of small group theory and research to social work practice.* New York: Columbia University Press.

Scheidlinger, S., ed. 1982. *Psychoanalytic group dynamics.* New York: International Universities Press.

Schwartz, W. 1974. The social worker in the group. In *The practice of social work,* ed. R. Klenk and R. Ryan, 208–28. Belmont, Calif.: Wadsworth Publishers.

Shorkey, C. 1979. A review of methods used in the treatment of abusing parents. *Social Casework* 60: 360–67.

Wayne, J., and K. Weeks. 1984. Group work with abused adolescent girls: A special challenge. *Social Work with Groups* 7 (4): 83–104.

Yalom, I. 1985. *The theory and practice of group psychotherapy.* New York: Basic Books.

Zalba, S. 1967. The abused child: A typology for classification and treatment. *Social Work* 12 (Jan.): 70–79.

6

Out-of-Home Care: Family Foster
Care and Residential Treatment

Burt Shachter, Ed.D.

Introduction

A primary responsibility of helping professionals working with maltreated children and their families is to prevent placement wherever feasible. Placement of a child outside of the home is one of the most radical interventions. Clearly, a request for placement signals a crisis in the life of the family. Sometimes intense work by the clinician can avert placement.

There are occasions, however, when placement cannot be avoided or when preplacement preventive work is insufficient, unavailable, or strongly resisted. Placement of a child out of the home is indicated as a last resort when the child is in serious danger. It is generally necessary when a child is subjected to unrelenting and unmodifiable physical or sexual abuse that endangers his or her physical or mental well-being. The nature of the danger must be verifiable and convincing to court personnel who have the ultimate responsibility for making decisions about placement. Placement is also indicated in situations of substantial, chronic, and unremediable neglect, often found with parents who suffer from severe mental disturbance or substance abuse.

The worker must decide not only whether to remove a child from the home, but what type of placement would be appropriate.

This chapter will describe available placement options, the criteria for selecting one, and the goals of placement. Selected aspects and problems in the placement process with the child and family will be discussed and illustrated by brief case vignettes.

Guiding Criteria for Differential Placement

Differential criteria for selecting placement options are necessary to ensure that these critical decisions are not determined arbitrarily, colored by agency bias, or controlled by the availability of community resources. Among the placement options are:

1. family foster care/group homes;
2. residential treatment programs (protective-structured and transitional-community-based);
3. psychiatric hospitalization.

Family Foster Care and Group Homes

Children suitable for family foster care should be emotionally capable of meeting the normal expectable requirements of family life. Children who have received good-enough parenting and are temporarily placed in foster care due to a family crisis often do well. But children who have been abused are often so developmentally damaged and distrustful that they are incapable of receiving or giving affection, and they require specialized programs. Most foster parents seek some emotional reward for their investment. They look for appreciation and love from the children they devote themselves to and are likely to feel defeated by distrustful, provocative, and distancing children. In some cases, specially selected and trained foster parents can work with these more disturbed children.

Fish (1984, 214)) considered family foster care inappropriate for children whose behavior "would not be tolerated in a community," children displaying "severe and unpredictable aggressive behavior." However, many abused children in foster care do fit this description.

Sometimes, it is possible to maintain one of these youngsters in foster care either if the foster care worker works closely with the foster parents or, if this is not possible, the foster parents are seen in a social agency. A case example will illustrate.

The Pattersons were foster parents caring for an abused child, Robert. They complained that no matter what they did for Robert, he continued to be distant, angry, and aggressive. They seemed disappointed because Robert gave them no returns for the effort they put out in caring for him. The foster care worker met with them regularly and impressed on them what a difficult and important job they were doing for Robert. The worker also emphasized that it was not a reflection on them that Robert did not show them love. The worker asked how Robert could be expected to show affection, no matter how well he was now treated, when he had not been given love all of his life. In this way, the worker provided the foster parents with appreciation and recognition so that they needed less gratitude from Robert.

For moderately troubled children, especially for those past puberty, small community-based group homes with specially trained parent-surrogate staff often prove more suitable. Staff who do not have twenty-four-hour-a-day responsibility are better equipped to tolerate the problematic behavior that would disturb natural or foster parents. Group homes can more readily provide for liaison with educational programs flexible enough to adapt their learning expectations to the cognitive and behavioral capacities of more emotionally damaged children and adolescents. At the same time, children in group homes can experience the same difficulties as those in foster homes.

Tom was a provocative, angry, aggressive youngster who irritated a staff person named Stan. Stan felt Tom had a chip on his shoulder and Stan wanted to put him down. He reacted aggressively to Tom, threatening him verbally and calling him names. Tom became increasingly defiant and dared Stan to hit him. Stan nearly did so, but fortunately another staff person in close proximity intervened. The advantage of the group home setting in this situation was that the other staff could see that Stan had difficulty dealing with Tom, and another staff member who was more tolerant was selected to approach Tom if a problem arose.

Residential Treatment Programs

Ideally, a residential treatment program should have the following components:

1. a controlled living environment geared to the growth and therapeutic needs of children;
2. individual, family, and group treatment in various combinations;
3. a flexible school program with strong remedial features; and

4. a well-trained interdisciplinary staff with the ability to tolerate disturbing behavior and the flexibility and sensitivity to avoid getting involved in the rejecting-abandoning behavior that severely abused children often provoke in caretakers.

A program encompassing all of these features is rarely available. But assuming that a reasonable program can be found, the following criteria should be considered in selecting maltreated children appropriate for these programs.

1. The child and family have failed to gain from previous nonresidential treatment. Or they have been persistently unable to avail themselves of such opportunity. In any event, the abuse has not been curtailed.
2. Continued presence of the child in the family milieu indicates ongoing obstruction of the youngster's development or deterioration that would not be altered by existing nonresidential therapeutic possibilities.
3. There is no adequate community-based school or alternative daytime environment that can tolerate the child's behavior and provide for cognitive social learning.
4. There is an antagonistic community, which cannot tolerate the child's behavior or presence.
5. Prior effort at foster care was unsuccessful.
6. The child's disturbed behavior pattern is not conducive to effective fostering by naturally selected surrogates without special training and qualifications.

To sum up this list of criteria, residential treatment programs should be considered when the family situation is untenable, the child's behavioral difficulties have reached a point that the community cannot tolerate them, and the community resources are not sufficient to help the child. Community resources might be insufficient because the child's difficulties are too severe or because the community lacks such resources.

Troubled children who do well enough in structured protective environments away from the mainstream of life run the risk of excessive institutional dependency and may then be unprepared to enter the real world. Children in mid or late adolescence who cannot return to their families may require a community-based residential facility specifically designed to facilitate the transition to independent living. Transitional facilities can also serve adolescents who outgrow or can no longer survive troubled natural family life or troubled family foster homes. The emphasis of the transitional facility is to prepare the adolescent for the tasks of living in the community through career training, employment experience, and the fostering of independent living skills such as money management, securing and maintaining an apartment, shopping, and cooking. These programs provide counseling to help prepare residents for independent living.

Psychiatric Hospitalization

For severely disturbed maltreated children and adolescents, psychiatric hospitalization may be the program of choice. This option is best for those unable to cope with even the most minimal demands of natural family foster home living, schooling, or community life. Hospitalization may be especially appropriate for those who are suicidal or homicidal or whose severe aggressive/assaultive behavior may require an even more structured and less pressured environment than residential treatment programs ordinarily provide. For these individuals hospitalization can be long- or short-term, ideally depending upon the assessment of the child and his treatment needs. Unfortunately, the length of hospitalization is frequently determined by the dictates of hospital insurance, limited to short, defined periods such as sixty or ninety days.

Residential treatment centers and family foster homes often use psychiatric hospitalization episodically when troubled youngsters experience psychotic crises that exceed staff tolerance and ability to guarantee the child's safety or the safety of others. Hospitalization can serve as a form of limit setting by providing an interim calming environment that can permit the reestablishment of coping resources and eventually the return to residential treatment or the foster home.

Gilbert was a youngster who had been severely abused by his mother. He was placed in residential treatment after being aggressively provocative and disruptive in school. In residential treatment, he became increasingly withdrawn. The other kids said he was different and "crazy." He refused to undress because he did not want to show how he had cut himself all over with a knife. The most severely disturbed abused youngsters often manifest psychiatric problems through self-abuse and mutilation. Gilbert had to be placed in a psychiatric hospital for his own protection. He was eventually discharged to a more protective residential treatment program that specialized in vulnerable, withdrawn, fragile youngsters as opposed to acting-out, aggressive children.

The Goals of Placement

There has been a growing professional consensus that it is important to minimize traumatic disruptions and re-placements in child caretaking. Abused children in foster care sometimes suffer the profound disruption of a move from one set of foster parents to another because the troubled children often provoke the rejection that they expect to find. Some abusive biological parents also surrender children under one set of circumstances only to reclaim them precipitously in times of loneliness, guilt, or impulsive whim.

The impetus for continuity of care and the concomitant movement toward legal permanency came largely from the influential work of Goldstein, Freud, and Solnit (1973). According to these authors, "primitive and tenuous first attachments form the base from which any further relationships develop" (18). Where basic needs (body comfort and gratification, affection, companionship, and intimacy) are regularly met, the child's intellectual and social development can be ensured. Inadequate and unreliable parental care impairs mental growth. The implication for placement is that it should offer or lead to consistent, dependable caretaking with as little disruption as possible.

In considering the goals of placement, there are four prevailing options:

1. placement as an interlude;
2. placement toward early permanency;
3. placement as a transition to independent living; and
4. protective care beyond childhood years.

Placement as an Interlude

It should be made clear to parents that placement is temporary. It is best to make a contract with the family and child that indicates that the agency is granting the family a vacation from its over-whelming childrearing burden. The respite period, usually of rela-tively short-term duration of six months to a year, is used for intensive family and individual therapeutic activity. The aim is the reintegration of the child and family. A desperate and abusive parent could gain respite and help that precludes striking again.

There are placement situations, however, that are likely to be long-term based on careful assessment.

Placement Toward Early Permanency

In some instances, the capacity and motivation for biological parents to resume childrearing responsibility is clearly in question. With termination of the rights of biological parents in selected in-stances and more enduring commitments from adoptive parents, one can reduce traumatic disruptions and facilitate growth in a more stabilized situation. Parents need skilled help in surrendering parental rights, and foster parents who serve well in the fostering role need time to consider whether they want to take on the life-long commit-ment of an adoptive parent.

Placement as a Transition Toward Independent Living

Many children literally grow up in foster care. Families may remain too disturbed, abusive, and neglectful, or they may simply disappear. In some cases, rehabilitation services to families of foster care children may be all too meager. There is also indication that children who have been in foster care for five years or more are often emotionally disturbed unless they have adequate treatment services (Frank 1980). A large number of foster care children who are precip-itously discharged from foster care directly to the community become inmates of prisons and mental hospitals and are among the homeless living on the streets or in fleabag welfare hotels. All of the above points show the need for small, community-based group homes or residential clubs to prepare for independent living. Too often, institu-tional dependencies are fostered and preparation for independent living becomes a frenzied afterthought when child welfare funding runs out, usually when the child is between eighteen and twenty-one years old

Protective Care Beyond Childhood Years

Some severely damaged foster care children or childhood psychotics who never master survival skills often are unable to cope as adults and are unable to hold mainstream jobs, maintain apartments, or manage money. Some of these return to destructive, abusive families, while others find their way into psychiatric hospitals, where they become revolving door residents. These children may have made impressive gains within their limited capacities but still cannot live independently. It is this group of former foster care children in need of life-long protective care for whom social welfare policy, funding, and political solvency are dramatically lacking.

Therapeutic Intervention

The following sections will discuss intervention in relation to the process of placement, foster care, and residential treatment. Special problems and clinical interventions will be outlined in all of these areas and illustrated with brief clinical vignettes.

The Placement Process

General Intake Considerations. Families will often be driven by desperate circumstances to seek placement, but at the same time they see it as a profound threat. Some may feel coerced into placement by the court and protective service authorities. Inconsistent approach-avoidance behavior on the part of parents is common. One day they might desperately plead for a child to be placed, and days later they will insist that the problem is resolved and placement is unnecessary. They often see the worker as judging, indicting, and rescuing. Themes of "Do something, I can't take it anymore" are often followed by accusations of "You want to take my child away—you think I'm a bad parent."

How the Worker Initially Helps the Family to Effect Placement.
The intake worker usually coordinates the evaluation for placement.
A typical evaluation includes a diagnostic psychiatric interview with
the child and parents, psychological testing of the child, and a psychosocial assessment of the family by the intake worker.

During the intake process, assessment and intervention always go
hand-in-hand. For instance, a parent presents a desperate plea for
placement of the child. If the worker readily joins in the placement
plan and zealously begins the arrangements, the parents will often
respond by suddenly changing their minds and accusing the worker
of trying to take their children away. This special problem will be
illustrated with a brief clinical vignette. Principles of effective intervention will then follow describing how the worker might respond to
this special problem

Ms. Anderson, a black woman, was abandoned by her paramour, Joe, and
took out her anger and frustration on her son Mike, who resembled his
father, Joe, in appearance. Ms. Anderson lost control and hurt Mike in an
abusive episode. She informed the child protective worker, Ms. Z., that she
was out of control and the child needed to be placed out of the home. Ms. Z.
began vigorously to pursue placement. To the worker's surprise, the mother
changed her mind and protested that Ms. Z. should not butt into her busi-
ness, adding, "You will take Mike over my dead body." Ms. Z. felt unappre-
ciated and angry in turn and directed all of her sympathies toward Mike,
whom she wanted to save from his "bad mother."

This vignette illustrates how the worker can get too caught up in
vigorously responding to the parent's overt request and lose sight of
underlying fear. All too often, when the worker immediately joins the
parent's request to place a child, the parent then turns on the worker,
accusing her of taking away the child.

Principles of Intervention in the Placement Process. If a parent
requests placement, the worker should not immediately agree, unless
the situation is an emergency in which the child is in immediate
physical danger. The worker should explain that placement might be
indicated but that only a full evaluation will determine the most
effective plan to help the child and family. The worker should emphasize that placement is one of several options, and that the purpose of
placement is to help and not punish the child and family with their

specific problems. Toward this end, the family is told that their cooperation and willingness are an important ingredient to any helping plan. If a parent comes in angry and seeking to place a child as an abandonment or punishment, it is especially important that the worker convey the view that placement is to help and not to punish.

Mrs. Matos went to a placement agency pleading that her daughter, Carmine, be placed in a "home." She said her daughter did not obey and that she could discipline her only through physical force. The worker replied that a full evaluation was necessary to determine whether placement or some other plan would best help the family. The worker added that a plan could not work unless she came to know the family better. The mother was told that the practitioner would work with the mother and child toward peaceful coexistence until the evaluation was completed. The worker also added that their work together might even prevent placement. The mother looked visibly relieved by the worker's cautious response.

Even where placement is involuntary, some degree of voluntarism in the placement process is desirable. With older children—especially adolescents—one should attempt to arrive at some level of participation in the placement work. The child or adolescent can be helped to participate by preplacement visits and meetings to foster care facilities or residential programs. These visits can reduce the threat of going off to strange, unfamiliar people and surroundings. Where court authority is being used to force the parent to place the child, the parent's cooperation and involvement should still be sought by the worker.

Mrs. Rush was forced by the court to place her abused child in a diagnostic center until a suitable residential long-term placement was selected. The worker involved her in the placement by asking the mother to visit the various residential treatment programs that were being considered. The mother was told that her opinion as to which facility would best serve her child was one of the factors that would be considered in arriving at a decision.

Whether placement is voluntary or involuntary, it is essential for the worker to provide the family with strong guilt- and fear-reducing professional guidance. The worker should explicitly explain as often as necessary that placement is a helping plan and not synonymous with abandonment or punishment. The parents need to have this fact spelled out to them.

Mrs. Thibaut had been changing her mind about placing her son for several weeks. She was plagued with doubt and indecision, worrying that he'd be badly influenced by other boys, that the food would be bad, and that she'd be abandoning him. The worker emphasized the temporary nature of placement and did not dismiss her concerns but instead helped her to take an active part in selecting a residence suitable for her child. The worker said it was good that she raised all of these questions and concerns because it showed that she cared about her child and did not want simply to get rid of him or abandon him but wanted to find a place that could help. In this way, the practitioner addressed her underlying fear and guilt by supporting her explicit concerns.

The intake process usually requires both individual and family interviews. Some children who become mute in the presence of the parent will be much more open in an individual meeting. A parent may also be less defensive in discussing abusive behavior without the child present. Family sessions are used to learn about the family interaction, which is often not apparent in separate interviews that can more easily conceal the interactional problems. Family meetings can also serve to clarify the purpose of placement. The worker can help family members confront their distorted perceptions of each other regarding the request for placement.

The capacity of the intake workers to remain in touch with personal feelings, biases, and judgmental attitudes within themselves is crucial. They need to be wary of tendencies to rescue the child from the "bad" parents, so that the parents are not further alienated from the treatment plan. Or conversely, for entirely different reasons, the workers must be careful not to join the parents in anger at the "bad system," which supports their denial of their own abusive behavior or the need for placement.

Intervention and Foster Care Placement

As Bowlby (1951) noted, placement is more successful when both child and natural parent accept it. But even where the parent(s) initiate placement with the seeming acquiescence of the child, this acceptance is relative and rarely unconflicted. Certainly younger children do not easily understand placement.

The reactions to placement depend greatly on the child's age and experiences and the circumstances in which placement occurs. The fantasies and feelings are acute and varied: dejection (they don't want or love me); guilt (they got rid of me because I was bad); hostility (I hate them and never want to see them again); fear of the unknown (will the new people want me, take care of me); shame (why are my parents so crazy or incompetent that they can't care for me like the parents of other kids do). A most haunting, anxiety-evoking, depressing reaction concerns anticipated abandonment and permanent loss. The fantasized questions might include: "Will they take me back? When? What will happen to them while I'm away? Who will replace me? Will my parents disappear?"

Family foster care children need skilled social work services even in coping with the situational crisis of temporary placement. Interventions with children can be directed toward the array of troublesome and disturbed reactions described above. Techniques will vary with the child's age, verbal capacities, motivation, and placement circumstances. Nonetheless, some general principles can be drawn in intervening with maltreated youngsters in foster care.

General Principles of Intervention with Maltreated Youngsters in Foster Care

The foster care worker can begin by asking the child to discuss his or her understanding of the reasons for placement. The worker might say, "What do you know about why you had to leave your parents and live for a time with the Williams family?" Children might present any of the reasons described above, such as the parents did not love them, wanted to be rid of them, thought they were bad, and so on. The worker should correct the child's misperception without describing the parent as bad but rather by emphasizing the parent's inability to take care of the child.

Gilbert, a ten-year-old child, told the worker that his mother always said that he was "bad" and that she'd throw him out in the street. He said his mother finally sent him away. The worker explained that his mother always called him bad because she had problems that upset her and that she was getting help with these problems so she could take better care of him. Gilbert listened attentively, so the worker asked if he had any idea of what was meant by problems. Gilbert wondered if the worker meant that his mother drank every day and walked around talking to herself.

Young children will often express problems, past traumas, and tensions through play activity, storytelling, and picture drawing. If the worker provides the child with dolls or puppets and picture-drawing materials, the child will often spontaneously play out past abusive traumas and current fears. For instance, one constricted youngster, John, could not talk to the worker about the experience that resulted in placement, but he spontaneously picked up dolls and enacted a parent abusing a child and sending him away forever. The worker was then able to comment on how frightened John was and how he feared his mother had abandoned him. John listened attentively and seemed relieved at expressing his fears and being understood.

Some maltreated youngsters exhibit provocative and destructive behavioral problems even with nurturing, stable foster families. These children, as well as youngsters requiring long-term placement or transition to permanent adoption, are candidates for ongoing counseling and therapeutic help. Some foster care agencies will refer these children to mental health clinics or family treatment agencies. That so few family foster children in need receive such help (Frank 1980) must be recognized and addressed by policy makers. The children in question need a more intensive form of treatment toward overcoming resistance to placement, so that the family foster care enterprise is not subverted. The child may fantasize that bad behavior will destroy the placement and necessitate a return to an idealized absent natural parent. In such cases, a complex form of treatment aims at working through abandonment depression and the psychic pain of being unwanted that ordinarily precedes or accompanies new reparative relationship investments with the worker, with foster parents, and with others. Ultimately the child may need help in defining or redefining the future. The child must come to terms with who the biological parents are, why they couldn't continue to provide care, and what kind of relationship with them (for better or for worse) is possible. The process of de-idealizing, which is normally a part of all child development, can be precipitous and traumatic for the maltreated child. Helping the child face the limitations of natural parents can be balanced by accepting the good parts of the parent even though such good parts may be meager. This form of intensive long-term treatment requires a very skilled and experienced clinician.

Intervention Principles with Foster Parents of Maltreated Children

The match between the maltreated child and foster parent(s) is rarely ideal. The foster parent may seek a child who will reciprocate affection and reduce loneliness, while the child is too traumatized and distrustful to respond to such expectations. If the placement is based on careful assessment, such disparity can be ameliorated. However, it is very difficult to find a foster family that can tolerate the behavioral problems and provocations maltreated children often exhibit. Numerous special problems are common to the foster care of maltreated children. Some youngsters tend to view the natural parent(s) as all "good" and deny their anger over the abuse and neglect they have experienced. Then they will vent their anger and frustration on the foster parents, whom they view as "all bad." In such instances, the child often has rescue fantasies that the natural parents will prove their love by saving the child from the "all bad" foster parents. In other cases, the maltreated child may provoke the foster parent into reacting as the original abusive parent had. These types of cases require individual intensive treatment of the child. The foster parents will need much support, empathy, and encouragement from the worker. In general, foster parents looking for appreciation, love, or companionship from the maltreated child will come to feel disappointed even with those children who are not too severely disturbed because they are typically too needy to be very giving toward the foster parents.

The foster care worker can provide support and empathy by explaining to the foster parents the crucial role that they fulfill in providing the child with a safe temporary haven and by confirming to them how difficult it is to care for these children. In allowing the foster parents to ventilate about how the maltreated child is difficult to care for, the worker provides an avenue to express frustration and anger so that they do not have to vent these feelings on the child. Also, by providing them with validation and appreciation for their care of the child, the worker can lessen their need for these responses from the youngster.

There often is much role confusion in the relationship between social worker and foster parents. At times foster parents have been seen as *clients* to be treated or counseled; at other times they have been seen as *supervisees* to be supervised; and at still other times they have been regarded as *colleagues* with whom there is a more egalitarian collaboration.

Research (Fish 1984) shows that foster parents function more comfortably when they are treated respectfully as fellow collaborators, as colleagues rather than clients. In speaking of foster parents, Wolins (1963, 396) observed that role confusion is minimized "when they understand others' expectations of them to be no different from those of a natural parent." Young social workers, with no parenting experience of their own, can be held suspect when they appear prematurely as the advocates of the foster child and do not empathize with the difficulties of serving as substitute parents for often mistrustful or hard-to-rear children.

It is important that foster parents be helped to see the *temporary* nature of their role when temporariness in fact prevails. They need much support in the difficult mission of gaining a child's trust and affection only to see the child return to the biological parents. The rhythm of terminating old investments and starting anew with other foster children has its own concomitant roller coaster of emotions. They may need guidance in understanding how past trauma can influence current foster child reactions in troublesome ways. These foster parents may need guidance in reading the defensive purpose of the child's behavior. Of course, a collaborative model of social worker–foster parent cooperation presumes foster parents are sufficiently free of disturbance and adequately equipped to parent.

Principles of Intervention with the Natural Parents of Foster Children

Ordinarily, parents do not capriciously place their children in foster homes. They may do so in periods of intense crisis when their own coping capacities and childrearing potentials are overwhelmed by anxieties and situational difficulties. Or they may resort to longer-term placement because their own deprivations and abuse at the hands of their own parents resulted in revisiting with their children the trauma experienced in their own lives. Substance abuse, criminality, and prostitution are frequently found among parents who place their children with others. Unwed mothers often seek babies in the hope that the empty void in their own lives will be filled. Parents who maltreat their children can be very immature emotionally. When their children in fact do not gratify but seek independence through expectable oppositional or defiant behavior, these immature parents feel abandoned and rejected and can turn on their children.

Whether the objective is to help parents ride out a crisis on a short-term placement basis, find new ways of reestablishing a more growth-enhancing family life, simply not undermine the placement, or ultimately accept termination of legal parent rights, contact between social worker and biological parent can be crucial. Natural parents should never be judged. When their capacities are overwhelmed by personal traumas, they require empathic understanding. A good-enough social worker will not play the condemning, abandoning role anticipated.

Natural parents safely connected to a helping person are at the least much less likely to sabotage their children's placement. Those biological parents capable of more intense personal counseling can get their own personal lives in order sufficiently to resume the care of their child. Ultimately, one hopes to help curtail their abuse and neglect, to promote a greater capacity for effective parenting more attuned to the growth needs of their children as separate beings.

For many, social work intervention may promote a more stable, though limited, role for natural parents in the lives of their children. Or it may promote termination of parent rights in place of inconsistent, disruptive, traumatic episodes of reclaiming and abandoning their children in foster care. Too often, family foster care fails because natural parents are forgotten or presumed to be irretrievably "unworkable." Such presumptions can become self-fulfilling prophecies.

The following brief vignette will illustrate how empathic work with a natural parent supported the foster care placement.

Ms. Diaz voluntarily placed her abused daughter in foster care. She became remorseful and guilty, feeling that she abandoned the child. She went to the worker and demanded the return of the child. When the worker did not immediately respond, she accused the worker and agency of "stealing" her child. The worker did not become defensive but instead reminded her of the temporary nature of placement, discussed visits that could be arranged between the natural mother and child, and offered counseling for Ms. Diaz to help her prepare for her child's eventual return. These interventions helped the mother to play an active part in the placement and to feel less guilty about abandoning her child.

Interventions and Residential Treatment

Unfortunately, not all residential settings actually provide treatment. Residential treatment should embody, at the very least, a living environment that is not noxious. At its best, it will use all available components of the living situation, clinical processes, education, and recreation in an individualized treatment plan suitable to the specific needs of the child. Interdisciplinary staff must collaborate, plan, and problem solve to provide a growth-enhancing therapeutic milieu attuned to the assessed needs of the child in placement. They must refrain from reacting with the destructive behavior that maltreated youngsters can sometimes provoke, and they must struggle to overcome staff conflict that is induced by the children. If the staff can face conflict, resolve it, and remain united in addressing the needs of the children, the residential milieu can have a powerful therapeutic impact. The above description represents the ideal of what residential treatment ought to be, but unfortunately it cannot be assumed that programs always meet this ideal.

Those children who are placed in residential settings are usually much more troubled than their counterparts in family foster care. In fact, many may have failed in one or more foster homes. They are more likely to act out destructively or self-destructively and to tax the patience and good will of those who care for them. They require firmer external structure and limit setting. If the staff is not given special training and adequate supervision to manage these difficult children, they can easily fall into punitive and rejecting reactions that replicate the behavior of the abusive parents. The worker effecting the placement of a maltreated youngster has a responsibility to select a residential program that can meet the special needs of the youngster.

Stages in the Postplacement Process

After the child has been placed, defensive maneuvers on the part of the child and family toward undoing or disrupting placement may continue for a long while—from several months to a year or more. Referring especially to residential treatment, Rinsley (1980) usefully depicted the stages of placement as roughly equivalent to Bowlby's (1960) three stages of an infant's reaction to separation: protest, despair, and detachment. Rinsley referred to these stages for adolescents in placement as *resistance, depression,* and *chronicity.* The professional helper's task is to enable the child and family to confront and work through resistance and to help them see its self-destructive consequences. This can enable them to face the losses involved in placement. The aim is to avoid the chronicity or pervasive detachment of a possible third stage. Since residential treatment more often involves court action or a more coercive component than does foster care, the resistance stage can be far more intense. One often faces a desperately unhappy child who expresses resistance through destructive behavior and actions. The child's enacted protest against the residential program challenges the tolerance of the interdisciplinary team. The clinician must be skillful in intervening with the child and in helping cottage parents manage destructive, provocative behavior.

Jimmy was a thirteen-year-old boy who played the social worker and cottage parents against one another in the initial phase of residential placement. He would provoke the cottage parents to become punitive and rejecting and then give the social worker a blow-by-blow description of the cottage parents' inappropriate behavior. Jimmy was quite adept at pinpointing the weaknesses in people and provoking them to react in the most negative way possible. The worker did not at first challenge Jimmy's all-bad view of the cottage parents, because he knew from past experience that the youngster would not readily give up his view. Rather, the worker focused on the child's destructive behavior. He would say that if Jimmy were right and the cottage parents were out to get him, what could Jimmy do to make himself less of a target? If Jimmy said that the cottage parents picked only on him for not cleaning his area, the worker replied that if Jimmy were right, then it was all the more important that he clean his area and not leave himself open to be picked on. The worker would say, "If you believe they are out to get you and you do not clean your area, you want to be picked on. If you clean your area, you don't want to be picked on."

Principles of Intervention in the Treatment of Acting-Out Youngsters in Residential Placement

The interventions in the case of Jimmy were directed toward his actions. Maltreated acting-out children express feelings and thoughts through action, so interventions must be directed toward their behavior. It will be noted that the worker did not challenge Jimmy's perception of the cottage parent as "all-bad." In this early phase of treatment the youngster makes his new parent figures "all-bad" and protects his biological parents as "all-good." The child is not yet ready to give up this all-good and all-bad way of thinking. Therefore, the worker accepts the child's basic world view and intervenes within that context. The worker accepts Jimmy's need to see the cottage parents as all-bad, but then says that *if* Jimmy is right and they are out to get him, then Jimmy can either behave in a way that results in their mistreating him or avoid behavior that will get him into trouble. The goal is for Jimmy to say to himself, "Wait, if I behave this way they will punish me—is that what I want?" Jimmy's need to view others as all good and all bad is a more complex, ingrained dynamic that is less accessible to intervention in the early phase of treatment. It will also be noted that the worker does not intervene with insight techniques, for instance by asking Jimmy why he would want the cottage parents to abuse him. The acting-out youngster is usually not ready to understand his motivation, especially in the earlier phases of treatment.

In the middle phase of treatment, when the youngster's acting-out behavior has significantly decreased, the worker might begin to identify the youngster's tendency to think in all-good and all-bad terms and to correct these distortions about people. However, this principle of intervention requires much skill and training on the part of workers and some capacity for insight on the part of clients. The giving up of the all-good view of others will lead to abandonment depression (the loss of the defensive belief that the abusive parent is all-good) and will require that children give up certain defensive illusions about their parents. Some severely disturbed children in residential programs never reach this phase of treatment but still make sufficient gains by lessening destructive, acting-out behavior.

The case of Jimmy was used to illustrate some principles in working with the destructive behavior of a child. However, the social worker must also work with the cottage parents in helping them to react therapeutically with the acting-out youngsters.

Some Principles of Interdisciplinary Collaboration in Residential Programs

Most of the children in residential treatment settings are prone to see their parents, themselves, and others as either all-good or all-bad. Developmentally, the capacity to experience oneself and others as whole but imperfect people has not yet arrived. In the context of an interdisciplinary staff there exists the potential for differential role delineations, which may foster certain problems. Child care workers or cottage parents handle day-to-day reality problems and must enforce curfews, rules, and work assignments. They are therefore often the recipients of the residents' hostility. They may envy the social worker's more permissive stance. Added to this is the child care worker's sense of lesser status in comparison with the social worker. This may set the stage for the child care person to act out his competitiveness with the social worker, to vie for being the recipient of the child's love. The child care worker may even encourage the resident's resistance to counseling in order to gain the resident's loyalty and become the sole positive protector. Conversely, the social worker may resent the easy comraderie that develops between a resident and a child care worker.

Some competitiveness is inevitable in a milieu where each resident works with more than one staff member. Different educational, racial, and socioeconomic backgrounds, as well as salary differentials, complicate the relationship of social worker and child care worker. This diversity can fuel the child's tendency to play one worker against the other. Such diversity, however, will not obstruct staff collaboration where open communication and problem solving among interdisciplinary staff is effective. Under the best of circumstances, a collective narcissism prevails. This means either staff succeed together in helping the child or they fail together. Individual competition is disavowed and avoided. This state of affairs reflects an ideal but can not be taken for granted or considered universal in residential programs. A short clinical vignette will illustrate the struggle of the social worker and cottage parents to collaborate in the residential treatment of a maltreated child.

Russell was a maltreated eleven-year-old who constantly provoked his cottage parents by disobeying rules and ridiculing them. The initial collaboration between the cottage parents and Russell's social worker resulted in an impasse. The cottage parents would complain about the youngster and the social worker would immediately defend him and make suggestions about how the cottage parents could more effectively manage him. They, in turn, questioned whether the treatment was helping. The collaboration was finally able to go beyond the impasse when the social worker was open to hearing how difficult it was for the child care workers to cope with Russell on a day-to-day basis. A significant shift occurred when the worker acknowledged that there were no easy answers to dealing with Russell's problems and that both the cottage parents and social worker were having a difficult time helping him. At this point, the cottage parents began to identify small signs that the social worker's treatment was taking some effect and they also could see evidence that their day-to-day limit setting resulted in small gains. The cottage parents and social worker began to feel that they were collaborating in a united effort to help Russell instead of competing with one another.

At other times, the disciplining style of cottage parents can be at variance with the needs of a particular child, and the social worker can be helpful in resolving the difficulty.

Mr. Gardiner had a drill sergeant style of managing his cottage. He spoke in a gruff tone and would sometimes pull rank on the boys to get them to follow his orders. Many of the youngsters liked him and were not sensitive to his brisk tone. Marvin, a sixteen-year-old youngster, had special problems with Mr. Gardiner. The boy had been severely maltreated and coped by having the attitude that no one would ever mistreat him again. He experienced Mr. Gardiner as abusive and reacted with hostility and arrogance rather than by "knuckling under." Mr. Gardiner, in return, decided that he was going to knock the chip off Marvin's shoulder. Marvin's social worker approached Mr. Gardiner about the problem. The child care worker insisted that Marvin's behavior was an affront to his authority and he would "get on" Marvin until the youth learned some respect. The social worker described Marvin's history and his refusal to knuckle under despite the abuse of his overpowering parents. Mr. Gardiner then said that he recognized himself as a youth in Marvin, that he too acted arrogantly and never submitted to authority. With the help of the social worker, Mr. Gardiner was able to turn his special interest in Marvin into a more positive, caring relationship. The social worker explicitly acknowledged the important role that Mr. Gardiner could play in Marvin's development.

These vignettes illustrate several basic principles in collaborative work. It is essential that team members acknowledge the importance of other team members in the helping process instead of viewing themselves as the sole helper and protector of the child. Child care staff play a crucial role in their parental position with the child, and social workers are important in terms of their specialized knowledge of personality, family, and systems dynamics. Before offering guidance and suggestions, it is essential that the social worker convey an understanding of the day-to-day problems with which other staff members must cope. Each staff member should also identify the small gains that other staff members help the very disturbed child to achieve. Sometimes, the frustrations and disappointments in daily work with a child can cause the cottage parent or social worker to lose sight of small but significant gains. Other staff members can help them keep their work with the child in perspective. The social worker should help the cottage parents become aware of the individualized needs of children based on their biopsychosocial familial development. The cottage parent can help the social worker perceive the child in a broader perspective based on every-day familiar contact with the youngster. The basic principle is that collaborative work should be a cooperative as opposed to a competitive effort. Admittedly, this view presents an ideal state of affairs and is not easily achieved in reality.

The Termination of Placement

Ideally, once the earlier period of resistance and acting out is confronted and limited, the child's underlying painful affects (loss, depression, anger, hurt, disappointment) emerge. The worker then helps the child deal with these feelings. If and when the affects are worked through, the child is freer to make use of new attachments in corrective ways, to get on with remedial education and other growth tasks necessary for resuming life in the outside community. Toward the latter part of residential treatment in particular, effort may be invested in redefining the relationship between child and natural parents.

For most of those placed in residential treatment, usually in their adolescent years, adoption is not a feasible goal. For significant numbers of others, neither is the goal of returning to live with biological parents a real option. The goal for those adolescents neither adoptable nor able to return to families of origin is of necessity independent living. Such a goal needs to be determined early and kept in view during the whole course of residential placement. Along with remedial education, therapy, and a corrective living environment, the resident must be prepared through the whole course of placement for concrete survival skills that facilitate independent living. The wherewithal for self-regulation (working, paying rent, managing money, cooking, and maintaining supportive relationship ties) must be addressed throughout and not left as an afterthought at the moment of discharge.

The preparation for reentry into the outside community may take place directly from the protected world of the residential setting or via transfer to the kind of transitional, community-based residential facility referred to earlier in this chapter. In either case the resident, under the best of circumstances, does well to redefine his or her relationship to natural parents. There is a "rapprochement crisis revisitation" (Shachter 1978) in transitional programs. This means that the child experiences conflicts around independence/dependence similar to that of the very young child. As actual discharge approaches and tangible signs of imminent adulthood become more visible, adolescents often take one more desperate flight back home in search of the elusive, omnipotent, all-good parents persistently wished for. They may, in response to the new sense of vulnerability that approaching independence brings, conflictually demand and fight to get the nurturance of which they have been deprived. Or, adolescents may revert to their very best behavior, assuming that since their badness has chased the parent away, their goodness can bring the parent back. They may seek to achieve the ideal, close, gratifying relationship with the parent that they never had. However, adolescents usually become disillusioned once again as their parents are unable to meet their needs and are the same as they were previously.

Having experienced a substantial dose of such disillusionment, adolescents may now be ready to use counseling for a more effective level of reality testing. If reality testing is attempted before a full measure of revisitation and disillusionment is experienced, it may prove useless. In some instances regressive forms of attachment will reemerge. The social worker or parent-surrogate staff member will be projected as totally bad while the parent at home becomes idealized.

In time, the social worker who waits out the process may find the disillusioned adolescent ready to look at options outside the family of origin. Where the reality-testing process does begin to work, adolescents can then be helped to redefine the kind of relationship with parents that is achievable. They can be helped to consider such questions as: "Can I have any relationship at all? If so, what kind is possible? What must my input into the new kind of relationship be?" Such a redefined relationship assumes a more realistic capacity to see the parent as a separate person with limitations and strengths. For many adolescents such redefinition may offer more security than the abyss of no contact at all with the family of origin. It may be the only kind of reconnection or rapprochement possible. Whether the resident physically returns to living with his family or is helped to live independently, such reconnection is important. With such redefinition of child-natural parent ties, the resident is less likely to replay the traumatic scenarios of the past in new, age-appropriate relationship endeavors as foster care or residential treatment is left behind.

References

Bowlby, J. 1951. *Maternal care and mental health.* Geneva: World Health Organization.

———. 1960. Grief and mourning in infancy and early childhood. *Psychoanalytic Study of the Child* 15:9–52.

Fish, S. 1984. Casework to foster parents. In *Child welfare: A source book of knowledge and practice,* ed. F. Maidman, 235–62. New York: Child Welfare League of America.

Frank, G. 1980. Treatment needs of children in foster care. *American Journal of Orthopsychiatry* 50 (2): 256–63.

Goldstein, J., A. Freud, and A. J. Solnit. 1973. *Beyond the best interests of the child.* New York: Free Press.

Rinsley, D. B. 1980. *Treatment of the severely disturbed adolescent.* New York: Jason Aronson.

Shachter, B. 1978. Treatment of older adolescents in transitional programs: Rapprochement crisis revisited. *Clinical Social Work Journal* 6 (4): 293–304.

Wolins, M. 1963. *Selecting foster parents.* New York: Columbia University Press.

7

Clinical Social Work Practice with Minority Families

Lucretia J. Phillips, D.S.W., and
Gladys Gonzalez-Ramos, D.S.W.

Introduction

Social workers counseling maltreating minority families must have cultural sensitivity toward the clients' cultural beliefs, values, practices, and traditions. Although there are many commonalities between minority and nonminority maltreatment cases, blindness to the impact of minority status may undermine the clinician's effectiveness in work with minority families.

This chapter will focus on the two minority groups with whom the authors are most familiar, black and Puerto Rican families. Maltreated children and their families are found among all socioeconomic, religious, racial, and ethnic groups, but it is widely recognized that low-income black and Puerto Rican families represent a disproportionate number of reported cases of child abuse and neglect. For example, in 1986 the New York State Child Abuse and Neglect register indicated that of 1,675 active maltreatment cases in New York City, 80 percent involved black and Puerto Rican families. These statistics make clear that certain aspects of the minority experience in America place poor blacks and Puerto Ricans at high risk for incidence of maltreatment. In their struggle to survive, these groups are particularly vulnerable to the multiple stresses that are often associated with child abuse.

Black and Puerto Rican Families

Though blacks and Puerto Ricans have similar experiences resulting from the lack of social justice, poverty, racism, and poor housing, and from lack of access to societal supports and resources (Phillips 1983), these two minority groups are quite diverse. In fact there are significant differences among various Hispanic groups as well.

The position of black Americans has been influenced by their African heritage, the conditions of American slavery, and the politics of exclusion (Phillips 1983). Discrimination, continuing barriers to social achievement, and the strain of trying to provide for the survival needs of family members have profound psychological impact on personality development, interpersonal relationships, and family structure. The black family is not traditionally patriarchal. Historically, the black father has been undermined in his position as provider as a result of slavery and limited economic opportunity. Hines and Boyd-Franklin (1982, 88) stated that black fathers' identity is associated with ". . . ability to provide for their families. Yet their chances for success in fulfilling this function are often limited because of discriminatory practices." Hill (1971) has emphasized the role flexibility that often occurs between black parents, as for example in child care, where mother and father might reverse roles if mother, and not father, is employed.

The black family often recognizes the need to prepare children to deal with discrimination, exploitation, and societal abuse while at the same time promoting their growth and development. "The strict, nononsense discipline methods of black parents are often characterized as 'harsh' or 'rigid' by mainstream-oriented observers" (Peters 1985). Corporal punishment, "getting a good whipping," can be perceived as abusive, but "firm control is important because many black parents experience anxiety about how their children will survive in this society. . . . they try to build in some controls so that the children are not placed in vulnerable positions, i.e., behaviors subject to misinterpretation" (Daniel 1985, 145).

Despite these stressors and their high vulnerability, many black families survive intact, drawing on many strengths they have developed, perhaps in part as a consequence of difficult life experiences. Among the factors that help black families function adequately are religious ties that offer many kinds of support, strong kinship bonds, and a strong work orientation (Hill 1971). In addition, in-group language and patterns of communication and a highly effective natural helping network in the black community—the local "Mom and Pop" store, the "number runner," the "brothers on the corner," and the host of other community folk—are all a part of the social climate that strengthens black families' ability to cope and survive (Phillips 1983).

Many of the issues relevant to the black family are also applicable to the Puerto Rican family. In addition, Puerto Rican families are affected by the disruption and other problems associated with migration, which is often forced for economic reasons, and the lack of support for resettlement. Anxieties emerge from adjusting to a new language and vastly different culture without familiar surroundings or customary support systems. Although legally Americans, they are often made to feel like intruders by the majority society and not like an integral part of American life. Limited opportunities and unequal access to resources impede the acculturation process and increase the sense of alienation. Dark-skinned Puerto Ricans are also subject to the same racial prejudice as blacks and may have feelings about their own skin color.

Unlike the black family, Puerto Rican families have been traditionally patriarchal. The husband as head of the family can make decisions without consulting his wife. The father expects a great deal of respect from other family members. "The husband is not expected to perform household tasks or to help with childrearing. This arrangement results in wives assuming power behind the scenes, while overtly supporting their husband's authority. This can work so long as she does not challenge him openly" (Garcia-Preto 1982, 170–71). Limited economic opportunities for the Puerto Rican father may result in marital stress when women are forced to seek employment, which threatens the self-image of Puerto Rican men and their sense of "dignidad" and "machismo." Consequently, there is a disruption of the traditional family organization and an erosion of the values that had served as a stabilizing force. Later, a clinical vignette will be presented that illustrates how these factors affecting the Puerto Rican family can lead to child maltreatment.

Like the black family, Puerto Ricans often emphasize strict disciplining of children to prepare them to deal with environmental hardships. "Puerto Rican culture teaches that a positive correlation exists between the degree of pain inflicted and the reduction of the incidence and scope of offensive behavior . . . failure to punish is shirking adult responsibility" (Hidalgo 1981, 5). Discipline maintains the valued concept of "respect." To have a badly brought up child implies failure of the parents to discipline the child properly. Physical and psychological discipline places limits on what the culture regards as unacceptable behavior. In disciplining, the psychological (verbal) can be as disturbing as the physical. Verbal exaggerations—employed to help displace the anger of the disciplinarian before or during the course of disciplining—represent a way to instill fear in those being disciplined without having actually to carry out the threat. "I am going to hit you until blood comes out" is an example. Other emotionally charged methods include threats of abandonment, humiliation, and withdrawal of love and support. If carried out, these behaviors constitute maltreatment regardless of culture or traditions. Verbalization, however, has to be evaluated in the context of a comprehensive assessment.

Puerto Rican families find much inner support from their extended families. The church too can provide desperately needed support and the sense of community that has been lost through migration. It is a gathering place where one can meet other families who share a cultural background and are subject to similar stresses. For many Puerto Ricans, spiritualism and the folk healer can also provide strength, support, and hope. Many mainland families may temporarily send their children back to Puerto Rico if they are experiencing difficult problems in order to draw on the extensive natural support system that exists there.

Assessment

In assessing black and Puerto Rican families living in inner-city neighborhoods, one must balance empathic understanding of the tremendous stresses under which they live with the primary need to protect the child. Using the broad biopsychosocial framework for assessment as outlined in chapter 2, the worker should emphasize the following areas in the assessment process:

1. stress and risk factors:
2. sociocultural background and values;
3. knowledge and mores regarding child development and child management;
4. ego functioning and coping mechanisms;
5. life cycle stages of family members.

Stress and Risk Factors

In assessing risk factors in minority families, workers should determine the presence and extent of:

1. substandard housing;
2. insufficient income or long-time unemployment;
3. chronic poverty;
4. single-parent family;
5. poor health;
6. substance abuse;
7. recent immigration or lack of acculturation;
8. absence of social supports;
9. poor education;
10. recent significant traumas;
11. indication of behavioral and developmental problems in the child;
12. crime and violence in neighborhoods;
13. severe emotional disturbance.

In dealing with these high-risk factors and stress overloads, each family has its own unique coping mechanisms. The social worker must assess the following factors:

1. How well does the family cope with stress?
2. Does stress overload affect the parents' ability to care for their child?
3. Are episodes of abuse triggered by stress? What kind of stress?
4. What supports exist that can help the family diminish or better cope with stress?
5. Do parents feel a sense of hopelessness?
6. How well does the family handle basic activities of daily living?

The answers to these questions help the worker plan interventive strategies, which are aimed at increasing the family's internal and external resources and thereby its ability to cope with stress, decreasing the nature of the stresses on the family, and developing nonviolent alternatives to managing stress.

It is especially important to note indications of substance abuse. Research and practice experience confirm that alcohol and drug use continue to rise at an alarming rate in poor communities and are significant contributing factors in many cases of child abuse (Research Utilization Update, January 1988).

Sociocultural Background and Values

Practitioners do not need to know all of the specific sociocultural characteristics and values of minority groups with whom they work, but some basic knowledge is necessary for full understanding of a client's behavior. Workers should be aware of:

1. those aspects of the culture in which the client takes pride;
2. culturally prescribed roles and expectations;
3. accepted childrearing practices;
4. attitudes toward problems and taking help;
5. valuable support systems;
6. religious and culturally sanctioned beliefs and practices.

Knowledge and Values Regarding Child Development and Child Management

Social class and cultural background influence the way parents raise their children. The practitioner must understand the childrearing methods of minority clients, particularly as they reflect cultural attitudes that are deeply embedded. The tasks for the social worker in terms of assessment are:

1. to ascertain the family's degree of understanding of children's developmental needs and how children should be raised;
2. to determine whether the family's understanding, attitudes, and behavior are appropriate to foster the child's growth and development;
3. to determine the family's motivation and capacity to expand their understanding and adopt alternative ways of managing their children.

Ego Functioning and Coping Mechanisms

The damaging deprivations and assaults experienced by poor minorities do not automatically create personality pathology. Despite the multiplicity of environmental stressors in their lives, many poor blacks and Puerto Ricans develop identifiable strengths and coping mechanisms. In order to appreciate these and to make an assessment of ego functioning, the practitioner must go beyond some of his or her own culturally biased or familiar concepts of normal or optimal ego functioning. The practitioner needs to explore the context in which the punishment occurred, the client's state of mind, the severity of the punishment, how similar or different this client is from other clients of a similar cultural background, and how the client behaves in other areas of his or her life. It is impossible for the practitioner to make an accurate ego assessment without considering what is an appropriate culturally based coping pattern.

The Life-Cycle Stages of the Abused Child

Sometimes, the parents will have problems dealing with the child at particular phases of his or her development and with the behavioral patterns the child manifests. For instance, a parent feeling overwhelmed by environmental stress might not have a problem when the infant can be easily quieted and calmed by having his or her physical needs met and naps for long intervals during the day. However, when the child is awake much of the time, begins to crawl, toddle, demand attention, and get into everything, the parent may then be overwhelmed and abuse the child when he or she demands excessive attention. Another parent might be very isolated, lonely, and threatened with loss when the child begins school. The parent may become angry at the child's natural striving for independence and enjoyment of outside activities such as school work or play with peers. The child's new-found pleasure outside of the home may trigger child abuse. Some minority parents may feel that environmental problems have impeded their opportunities to fulfill their hopes, ambitions, and aspirations. They might have unrealistic expectations that a child will fulfill the aspirations they could not achieve. When the child becomes an adolescent and does not fulfill the parents' "dreams," the parents might take out their frustration on the child. Of course, understanding the life cycle phases is only one factor in the comprehensive assessment of the family.

Intervention

In planning intervention strategies, the worker must begin by attempting to deal with the multiple stress factors that are nearly always present in poor black and Puerto Rican families. The intense frustration and anger that result are often vented on their children.

In treating these families, the worker must frequently provide nurturance to clients through supportive techniques that indicate concern and caring. The worker must be ready to reach out to these clients, to provide concrete services that ease reality burdens, to serve as the clients' advocate in negotiating various systems, and to encourage the clients to ventilate their anger. Actually, these methods of intervention are applicable to all maltreating parents. As Sager, Brayboy, and Waxenberg (1973) suggested, there is little in the treatment of a black person (or any other ethnic or racial minority) that is not common to all good therapy.

As mentioned in chapter 2, empathy, flexibility, and creativity are essential components in working with maltreating families; they are perhaps even more important with minority families who have already been involved with different agencies and have been disillusioned by an unreceptive staff or by conscious racist attitudes. The practitioner will need to engage in a broad repertoire of helping roles and techniques. This section will discuss:

1. the worker-client relationship;
2. outreach;
3. treatment modalities;
4. case management;
5. balancing treatment focus on the inner and outer needs of the family.

The Worker-Client Relationship

Among some of the potential difficulties in establishing a positive worker-client relationship with minority families are:

1. a lack of common language;
2. differing styles of nonverbal communication;
3. the differing expectations and understanding of the helping process;
4. the frequently diverse socioeconomic, ethnic, and cultural backgrounds of client and worker;
5. the practitioner's insufficient understanding of cultural factors;
6. conscious and unconscious racist attitudes on the part of the client or worker;
7. The fact that in child protective cases the workers represent institutional authority and power.

Work with minority clients requires creativity and flexibility in the professional use of self. To capture the essence of "where the client is" is a dynamic challenge for the practitioner. It enables the social worker to utilize cultural beliefs and behavior in establishing rapport with clients and a sharing of problem-solving tasks. There will be obvious cultural and/or class differences that influence encounters between clinicians and clients of widely different backgrounds. To prevent this difference from becoming insurmountable when relating to minority clients, the social worker must be open, direct, caring, and perceived as "genuine." The ability to hear the client, to give up myths and stereotypes about blacks and Puerto Rican clients, to ". . . perceive, understand and compare simultaneously the values, attitudes and behavior of the larger societal system with those of the client's immediate family and community system" (Norton 1978), are qualities that make productive engagement possible.

For example, in the treatment of Puerto Rican clients, small efforts, such as trying to learn a few words of Spanish (even when translators are used) or making a concerted effort to pronounce a client's name or nickname correctly, can go a long way toward evidencing a respectful, open, and interested attitude.

The ability to be genuine and open with minority clients and to respect differences is important in establishing the client/worker relationship. Regardless of how knowledgeable the worker may be, there are times when minority clients may hold certain cultural and religious beliefs and values that are unfamiliar to the worker. The worker must truly try to understand the client's point of view and should not feel embarrassed to ask about beliefs he or she may not understand. For example, the worker may find it surprising to encounter clients who practice spiritualism and difficult to understand how important this may be to them. Nonjudgmental inquiry helps clients recognize the workers' true interest and acceptance of their beliefs. By contrast, workers who subtly disparage beliefs that differ from their own risk antagonizing and eventually losing the client.

Social workers must be conscious of their own ethnic backgrounds as well as the client's, though it may not be necessary to deal with this issue directly. Actually, the client-worker relationship can be affected when the client and worker are of different ethnic and racial backgrounds as well as when they are of the same ethnic or racial background. Some brief clinical vignettes will illustrate the problems that might arise when the client and worker are of different ethnic backgrounds.

In the treatment of a six-year-old black boy, Walter, the issue of color differences emerged while playing the board game of "Othello" in play therapy. Walter always chose to use the black chip and assigned the worker the white chip. On one occasion, the worker reached for the black chip and the child said, "No, you are white."

The worker replied "You're right, I'm white and you're black. I wonder how you feel talking with someone white." Walter said he likes the worker because he is different from white schoolmates and teachers who pick on him. The worker plays with him, doesn't always try to win, and even teaches him how to play better. The worker wondered if Walter thought in the very beginning that he might not get along with the worker because he is white. Walter said he was afraid the worker would pick on him and even now he still becomes scared if he wins a game that the worker will get angry at him.

If the difference in ethnic background between client and worker seems to be problematic, the worker should directly raise the subject and ask the client whether he or she is comfortable talking to the worker. The practitioner should also inquire whether the minority client has had previous negative experience with other white social workers or authority figures. A brief clinical vignette will illustrate.

Ms. Tucker was a black single parent referred for treatment for abusing her children. She was at first guarded and hostile. The worker asked directly, "Are you uncomfortable talking to me?" The client admitted that she was not comfortable talking to a white worker and she doubted if the worker could understand her situation. The counselor did not attempt to convince her that she could understand but instead inquired whether Ms. Tucker had had bad experiences with other white social workers, teachers, or persons in authority. The worker said, "You will be able to see another worker if, after we talk about it, you still feel you can't work with me." The client seemed visibly to relax at this point as she took off her jacket. Ms. Tucker explained that her child's white teacher had accused her of being an abusive, neglectful parent and she expected the same treatment from the worker. She then said that as a result she anticipated that any counselor would judge her to be a "bad abusive mother." The fact that the worker was white compounded her fears. When she saw that the practitioner encouraged her to discuss her feelings and did not react punitively, she became less guarded and said she would at least try to work with the white worker.

Just as a minority client might express negative feelings about having a white worker, a minority client might express negative feelings about having a minority worker.

Ms. Monroe, a black woman, came to a family clinic because she had abused her child. She was assigned to a black worker. The clinic had a majority of white workers. She complained that she was assigned to a black worker because she herself was black. For the next few weeks, she would verbally abuse the worker in much the same way that she abused her child. For instance, she spoke of how the worker must be left out by other workers, how the worker was probably hired as a token black and was less skilled.

On one occasion, after being denigrated by Ms. Monroe, the worker said, "You know, the way you believe that I am mistreated because I'm black and that I'm inferior to everyone here makes me wonder whether you feel the same way about yourself. Perhaps during your life, you have been treated the way you believe I'm being treated." As the worker did not look hurt or retaliate but addressed the client's feelings about being black, Ms. Monroe began to recognize that the worker felt professionally secure, and she began to admire her.

This kind of intervention, which addresses the client's racial identity, requires great sensitivity on the part of the social worker and some capacity for self-observation on the part of the client. In most cases, it would be sufficient for the worker to discuss the client's feelings about having a white worker without making a connection to the client's feelings about being black.

Knowledge and sensitivity toward the client's sociocultural background promotes the worker-client relationship. Two clinical vignettes of a Puerto Rican and black family illustrate this point. The first shows how the social worker's knowledge and sensitivity to the role of the father in most Puerto Rican families played a important part in treatment.

The Diaz family consisted of the mother, Rosa, the father, Herberto, and a ten-year-old son, Jose. The father demanded a great deal of respect from the other family members and complained about the mother's overly close relationship to their son. He accused her of spoiling Jose and was jealous over the strong mother-son attachment. When the father lost his job, he became depressed at his inability to carry out the traditional role of provider. His intense frustration led to severe physical abuse of Jose. The worker's sensitivity to Mr. Diaz's feelings about losing his job enabled her to deal with the negative impact this had on his self-esteem and on his perception of himself as the head of the family.

The second case vignette illustrates the importance of the extended family in the treatment of maltreating black families.

Ms. Johnson was a black mother who sometimes mistreated her twelve-year-old son, Robert. She was unemployed, looking for work to support her family. Under great stress, she became increasingly impatient with her son's behavioral problems in school and began to beat him. The problems at home exacerbated Robert's problems at school, resulting in further maltreatment by his mother.

The family was referred to a social agency, where residential treatment was recommended for Robert. Ms. Johnson also thought that her son needed to get out of the home for a while, at least until she found a job and could provide for her family. However, she was opposed to residential treatment.

She had a plan to send Robert to her cousin's home until he straightened himself out and she was settled in a job. Her cousin was a strict but patient woman who, Ms. Johnson believed, would provide enough discipline and attention to "straighten him out." Her cousin had her own children who were doing very well. The cousin liked Robert and was willing to take him.

The social worker recognized that sending an acting out child to relatives or friends in another neighborhood was not unusual in Ms. Johnson's cultural milieu and did not imply lack of concern about the child. As Hines and Boyd-Franklin (1982, 90) stated about black families, "An aunt or grandmother may share the responsibility for child care. It is not even uncommon for a child to be informally adopted and reared by extended family members who have resources not available to the child's parents or who reside in an environment more 'wholesome.' Many clinicians automatically assume that such a practice is indicative of rejection on the part of the parent and that it is perceived as such by the child, without giving consideration to the positive aspects of this practice."

The worker realized that Ms. Johnson was making use of the extended kinship system to help her child and herself. When the worker explained this plan to the agency staff, there was much debate and concern about the appropriateness of the plan. It was feared that the child would feel rejected and act out even more. However, Ms. Johnson's plan proved to be effective. The social worker met periodically with the family to see how the arrangement was working out. Robert did much better at his cousin's home and Ms. Johnson eventually found a job and took her son back.

Outreach

Despite the multitude of stressors experienced by minority families who maltreat their children, there is underutilization of service. There are many reasons for this. The service delivery system is often unresponsive to the needs of minority client needs (Rogler et al. 1983). Specific agency barriers are:

1. insensitivity to cultural and language needs;
2. long waiting lists;
3. insensitivity to racial and ethnic issues;

4. geographic inaccessibility;
5. inflexibility of administrative or bureacratic policies (office hours, insufficient time to make home visits, etc.);
6. insensitivity to or negative bias toward lower-class minority clients.

Many minority families mistrust the services of social agencies because of these barriers. The social worker must therefore reach out to these families in creative ways to show concrete evidence of interest and concern.

In addition to such obvious changes as making services geographically accessible to clients, agencies need to employ a greater number of personnel who can identify with the clients' ethnicity and speak their language. In cases involving school-age children, the school can often be utilized as a point of entry for the delivery of services, since parents already feel a sense of connection to and familiarity with the school. Effective outreach requires the extensive use of home visits, which are invaluable in both assessment and treatment. They provide an unparalleled opportunity for psychosocial assessment. Seeing families in their own natural setting—often in crowded, dilapidated quarters but still making efforts to care for their children—can be very revealing. What at first may seem to be indifference to their children can be better understood in the light of the family's milieu and their consequent feeling of helplessness and powerlessness.

While home visits can be invaluable, the worker needs to be sensitive to the fact that some families see home visiting as an intrusion on their private living space. They would rather visit the agency than have someone make a judgment on how they live. Many clients still recall or have heard that in the past caseworkers would unexpectedly visit a family to "investigate." If a home visit is desirable, the worker must be sensitive to feelings and be ready to deal with them. In planning a home visit, the social worker should be guided by the following principles:

1. The worker should arrange an appointment that is convenient for the family. When this is not possible, the worker should at least let the family know when he or she is coming.
2. Child protection workers often do have a mandate to investigate the living conditions of the family. The family should be advised of this mandate directly and without hostility.

3. At times the worker may not be able to reach the family in advance of a court-mandated visit. In fact, workers from public child protection services are usually required to visit the home without notice to evaluate complaints of abuse and neglect.

Once in the home, the worker should not be unnecessarily intrusive and should recognize with the parents that the visit is necessary to ensure the protection of the child. The following example illustrates the basic principles of intervention in cases involving child abuse and neglect.

The Monroes were a black family consisting of a single mother and six children living in substandard housing. The child protection worker was directed to visit the family to see that the children were receiving adequate care. The worker was not able to inform the family beforehand of the visit. Upon arriving the worker said, "I know this feels like an intrusion but the court ordered that I must come and see if your children are alright." The worker met with the children, saw that they did not appear to be in distress, and then talked with the mother. In the course of the interview, the worker learned that she had a heart condition and that one of her children, Thomas, was seriously disturbed and had both learning and behavioral problems. The mother, who was overburdened, took out her frustrations by beating the child. The worker said, "I can see you are living with many problems that make you frustrated and angry and because of this, you let out your anger on your child. I will arrange for you to get help for your many problems, but you absolutely cannot continue to mistreat Thomas or he will have to be removed from the home. Let us plan for another visit." The social worker then helped obtain necessary health care for Ms. Monroe and arranged for a developmental assessment for Thomas.

Different Treatment Modalities

The authors, in their clinical work with black and Puerto Rican families, have found that clients respond much more readily to offers to be seen individually rather than in groups. Gonzalez-Vucci (1985) noted in her study of Puerto Rican mothers' preferences for services that "initial engagements should utilize an individual approach. . . . Mothers might, with increasing familiarity, then be more amenable to family group approaches. . . . Mothers emphasized the importance of privacy and their feelings of shame and embarrassment at feeling exposed or judged by others." The response was similar to the authors' experience with black mothers. Individual treatment with a worker is far less threatening than a group situation in which one's inadequacies might be exposed. For clients who are often emotionally as well as socially deprived, the opportunity to participate in a one-to-one relationship can be a nurturing and corrective experience. Bowles (1969) noted that in her work with more deprived mothers, the one-to-one approach was especially important. She combined individual treatment with home visiting, feeling that these mothers cannot be expected, at least initially, to come to the agency voluntarily. The one-to-one reaching out approach is necessary to break through their isolation and feelings of mistrust and suspicion. Individual treatment lets the worker encourage the client to verbalize pent up anger over reality burdens rather than taking out aggressive feelings on the child.

Ms. Hernandez was a thirty-four-year-old single mother experiencing multiple problems resulting from substandard housing, inadequate finances, unemployment, and the behavioral problems of her three children. She was referred for counseling for physical abuse of her youngest child. She expressed surprise when the worker did not scold her but instead asked her to talk about the problems she encountered in her daily life. The worker made it clear that Ms. Hernandez must stop abusing her child, but the worker also provided concrete help for her many reality problems. If Ms. Hernandez did not come for a session or call to cancel, the worker would call her and visit the home if she was depressed or unable to arrange for child care in order to come to the clinic. Ms. Hernandez began to find the counseling valuable because, as she put it, she had never before in her life had the experience of another person paying attention and listening to her as if she were important and her problems mattered. The worker also encouraged her to ventilate her anger about her difficult life situation.

In some cases, when severe social and emotional pathology is not present, individual guidance on how to handle a child's behavior can help to modify a parent's abusive pattern.

Mr. Ortega was the thirty-four-year-old Puerto Rican father of twelve-year-old Raymond. Although a man of considerable intelligence, Mr. Ortega had not had the opportunity to pursue his education. He had to quit school and work at a young age to support his family. He now had two jobs so that Raymond could attend a private school and fulfill the aspirations that Mr. Ortega could not achieve. He pressured him to study day and night and did not allow him to go out with his friends. The boy rebelled by "acting lazy" and not trying hard when taking exams. In this way, he retaliated against his father's pressure and demands. The father's severe disappointment impelled him to beat Raymond in an attempt to force him to work harder.

When a relationship of trust had been established, the worker helped Mr. Ortega by explaining, "What you're doing is having the opposite effect from what you want. Raymond is getting back at you by not doing his work. If you would let him go out with his friends once in a while, he would be less angry and would probably do better in school."

When appropriate, minority parents can also be seen in group treatment. Group treatment can provide the opportunity to learn alternatives to harsh punishment in disciplining children. Time- and goal-limited groups for parents with a specific focus (child management, stress reduction, development of parenting skills, family communication, and so on) appear to be the most successful form of group intervention. Parents are usually eager to get information from the "expert." When a semblance of group rapport develops, more substantive personal material can emerge and the group can move into a therapeutic phase. In group treatment, the members can sometimes confront one another about abusive behavior.

Mrs. Walker was an angry mother, bitter over abandonment by her husband and estranged from her family. She was referred for abusing her seven-year-old son John.

In group meetings on parenting skills, with six other black and Puerto Rican mothers in similar situations, Ms. Walker was the most challenging. "I just slapped Johnny, didn't know his lip would split, I got many a split lip, black eye, and bloody nose when I spoke back to my grandmother . . . how can you tell me it's not right?"

Before the worker could answer, Ms. Jones commented, "You'll find out how right it is when they take your kid from you." Other group members also chimed in that they were abused as children and didn't like it. Ms. Walker now began to think back about how her grandmother would beat her and how it made her feel enraged and helpless. She wondered if she were now taking out all of her anger on her child.

In conducting family treatment with minorities, it is important for the social worker to recognize the importance of extended kinship alliances (Hines and Boyd-Franklin 1982). For instance, black and Puerto Rican families are often involved with extended family members who are important sources of support and strength. "Particularly as one begins to examine parenting, the extent to which extended family involvement can promote family survival becomes more apparent. Relatives expect and accept reliance from one another in times of need"(Hines and Boyd-Franklin 1982, 90).

The Rush family were black and consisted of parents who were formerly drug abusers and two young children. The parents were quite immature, unable to care adequately for their children, and often physically abusive to them. The mother mentioned a maternal grandmother who lived in the community. Before removing the children from the home, the social worker called for a family session to see if the grandmother would be willing to take a more active planned role in the family's life. The grandmother attended the family treatment sessions, in which a plan was established for her to help the parents care for the children. The grandmother was willing to "supervise" the family and reported on the parents progress in caring for their children. She made sure that the mother bought food regularly and that the parents did not use physical violence on the children. As a result, the children were able to remain at home. Mr. and Mrs. Rush were helped to become more adequate parents.

Case Management

Case management is another important interventive strategy. A multiproblem minority family is often dealing simultaneously with various systems, such as the social agency, the clinic, and several health facilities. They may be receiving a host of services, which are often uncoordinated and sometimes duplicated or even contradictory. At other times, the family is not receiving a sufficient number of services. The social worker helping the multiproblem minority family needs a comprehensive perspective of the various biopsychosocial needs of the family. The worker and the family must establish a plan of action with clear and attainable goals. The worker helps the family implement the plan and coordinates the often multiple-service component.

Often, case management or linking a family to additional needed services becomes the entry point or may even be the main part of the treatment plan. To some clients, the "talking cure" seems insufficient. They may not have the capacity to focus on their child-rearing practices or their reasons for losing control when overwhelmed by anger and frustration.

Ms. Feliciano was a Puerto Rican maternal grandmother taking care of her three grandchildren. Raymond, the seven-year-old child, was referred to a special child development team working within the school, showing numerous signs of physical abuse and neglect. The maternal grandmother did not respond to repeated requests to come to school and discuss Raymond's behavior. The family was isolated and without strong community ties. The school worker made a home visit to assess the family situation. The social worker assumed a case management role, by initiating a full evaluation for Raymond. She later got him admitted to an after-school program and a neighborhood weekend program in order to give the grandmother some free time. The worker also helped to create a neighborhood support network by encouraging her to reach out to neighbors and friends. As Mrs. Feliciano saw the worker set up and coordinate these various services for her family, she became increasingly open to discussing her problems in caring for her grandchildren.

This brief vignette illustrates how case management and provision of concrete services serve as an entry point and important part of treatment. As the grandmother received some help with overwhelming day-to-day problems, she became better able to focus on the child's difficulties and to accept help at other levels from the worker.

Balancing the Focus Between the Inner and Outer Needs of the Family

Each family has a host of inner (emotional, both conscious and unconscious) needs and outer needs (for concrete environmental services). Since most maltreating minority families are poor and suffer from multiple problems, there may be a tendency to become overly involved in attempting to manage outer needs without responding to the inner needs. This tendency to focus on the delivery of coordinated concrete services may result in part from the workers' own difficulties in listening to or empathizing with a family's fear, despair, anger, or other intense feelings. There may be a need in working with such families to feel more "useful" by becoming a visible "doer." More often, both counseling and concrete services are needed. Some families may need one group of services more than the other. Some may need substantial improvement in their day-to-day living conditions before they are able to sit and talk and place their trust in a worker.

The social worker must have a great deal of role flexibility in addressing both the inner and outer needs of the client. This means that the worker will have to shift back and forth from a case-managing to a counseling role. Generally, in the initial phase of treatment, it is essential to provide concrete services and alleviate major environmental stressors, which then frees the family to focus on parent-child conflicts. The following case vignette will illustrate this principle.

The Garcia family consisted of the parents and four children of Puerto Rican background. The case was referred to the special services school team because one of the children, Juan, was being seriously physically abused. The worker learned, through a series of home visits, that the mother directed her primary attention to the mentally ill father and delegated the responsibility of the family to the eldest daughter, Ana. While delegating responsibility to the oldest daughter can be a common practice in many Puerto Rican families, in this case Ana felt overburdened and vented her anger by physically abusing Juan, the most difficult sibling, who appeared to be mildly retarded. The mother's traditionalist beliefs were to become a major source of growing hostility between herself and Ana, who was more acculturated and wanted less family responsibility and greater freedom. The mother also vented her anger on Juan.

While the need for counseling was not ignored, the worker felt that it was premature until some of the immediate environmental stressors could be alleviated. The worker assumed a case managerial function and coordinated the steps required for assessing and implementing Juan's special educational needs and improving the treatment program for the mentally ill father.

Once these major stressors were alleviated, the worker could focus on counseling with the mother and daughter to lessen their need to scapegoat Juan.

Summary

Clinical social work practice with minority families requires in-depth understanding of racial and cultural factors. This content must parallel the basic knowledge and skill needed for effective clinical practice with all client groups. The conceptualization of the unique professional role defined in the integrative perspective is particularly useful in assessment and intervention with minority families who maltreat their children. Special attention to the stresses and social assaults experienced by minority group members will enable the practitioner better to understand these clients and work effectively with them.

References

Bowles, Dorcas D. 1969. Making casework relevant to black people: Approaches, techniques, theoretical implications. *Child Welfare* 48 (8): 468–75.

Daniel, Jessica. 1985. Cultural and ethnic issues: The black family. In *Unhappy families*, ed. Eli H. Newberger and Richard Bourne, 145–53. Littleton, Mass.: PSG Inc.

Garcia-Preto, Nydia. 1982. Puerto Rican families. In *Ethnicity and family therapy*, ed. M. McGoldrick, J. Pearce, and J. Giordano, 164–86. New York: Guilford Press.

Gonzalez-Vucci, Gladys. 1985. Puerto Rican mothers' preferences for delivery of mental health services. D.S.W. Dissertation, New York University School of Social Work.

Hidalgo, Hilda A. 1972. Ethnic differences affecting the delivery of rehabilitation services to Puerto Ricans. In *Ethnic differences*, ser. no. 4, 1–17. Washington, D.C.: National Rehabilitation Association.

Hidalgo, Hilda. 1981. Child abuse and neglect: A Hispanic perspective. Paper presented at the First New Jersey Statewide Child Abuse and Neglect Conference, New Brunswick, N.J., Nov. 20. Proceedings: 1–20.

Hill, Robert B. 1971. *The strengths of black families*. New York: National Urban League.

Hines, Paulette, and Nancy Boyd-Franklin. 1982. Black families. In *Ethnicity and family therapy*, ed. M. McGoldrick, J. Pearce, and J. Giordano, 84–107. New York: Guilford Press.

Norton, Dolores G. 1978. *The dual perspective*. New York: Council of Social Work Education.

Peters, Marie F. 1985. Socialization in black families. In *Black families*, ed. Harriette Pipes McAdoo, 209–24. Beverly Hills, Calif.: Sage Publications.

Phillips, Lucretia J. 1983. A model for teaching minority content to field instructors: The integration of minority content in the field instruction curriculum. D.S.W. Dissertation, City University of New York, Hunter School of Social Work.

Research utilization update. Community Council of Greater New York. January 1988.

Rogler, Lloyd, et al. 1983. A conceptual framework for mental health research on Hispanic populations. New York: Hispanic Research Center.

Sager, Clifford, Thomas L. Brayboy, and Barbara R. Waxenberg. 1973. Black patient—White therapist. In *Dynamics of racism in social work*, 141–51. Washington, D.C.: National Association of Social Workers.

8

Intervention with Maltreating Parents Who Are Drug and Alcohol Abusers

Shulamith Lala Ashenberg Straussner, D.S.W.

Introduction

I have been abused by both of my parents for as far back as I can remember. My father was an alcoholic, and he would beat me for stupid stuff. He used to take me in supermarkets and make me steal steaks, and he would go in bars and sell them. Then he'd drink with the money he made. Once I got caught, and he beat the hell out of me and kicked me. . . . My mother beat me because she was angry. She had to go to work then and come home and cook and raise five kids, and she couldn't handle the pressure. Michael, 17-year-old drug abuser (*The New York Daily News,* October 6, 1981)

Clinicians and researchers have only recently recognized that growing up with a drug-or alcohol-abusing parent is frequently a highly traumatizing experience with long-lasting effects. When familial drug and/or alcohol abuse is compounded by child abuse, both assessment and intervention become increasingly complex. This chapter will examine the relationship between parental drug and alcohol abuse and child maltreatment. It will describe different types of substance abuse and their effects that may contribute to abuse and neglect. Then it will consider practice principles with this troubled population.

The Impact of Drugs and Alcohol Abuse on the Individual

In order to understand the dynamics of maltreating parents who are substance abusers it is important to clarify the numerous terms used in discussing individuals who abuse drugs and/or alcohol and to understand the impact of the various substances on the individual.

Technically, alcohol is classified as a mood-altering drug or chemical. Thus, terms such as *drug abuse, substance abuse,* and *chemical dependence* are frequently used synonyms that encompass both drug and alcohol abuse. For the purposes of this chapter, the term *substance abuse* will be used to encompass the abuse of both alcohol and other drugs, while the term *drug abuse* will generally refer to abuse of substances other than alcohol. The term *abuse* typically refers to the "chronic, compulsive use of a substance in such a manner that it assumes a central and negative role in the individual's lifestyle and results in impaired functioning. Included in this definition is the psychophysiological dependence on drugs or alcohol, i.e., psychological or physical addiction" (U.S. Department of Health and Human Services 1978, 56).

The terms alcoholism and drug addition commonly refer to the existence of both psychological and physical dependence on alcohol or narcotic drugs. They imply the existence of an initial increase of tolerance to the chemicals—more and more of the substance is required to achieve the same effect. Once tolerance has developed, the individual cannot wait too long between doses without experiencing physical withdrawal symptoms. Alcoholism also implies an eventual decrease in an individual's ability to absorb alcohol in the system—a decrease in tolerance, as well as a progressive deterioration of the individual's physical and mental status, including possible brain damage due to drinking (commonly referred to as "wet brain" syndrome) or even death. Although addiction to narcotics does not in itself cause death or illness, drug addicts experience numerous illnesses and infections. Death can result from using contaminated drugs or unsterile needles, from overdosing by unknowingly injecting a drug of higher potency than normal, or due to the harmful impact of combining heroin with other drugs. Currently, a growing number of drug addicts are dying of AIDS.

The recently revised Diagnostic and Statistical Manual (DSM III-R) put out by the American Psychiatric Association (APA 1987) differentiates between the *abuse of* and *dependence on* such substances as alcohol; sedative and hypnotic drugs; inhalants; opioids; cocaine, amphetamines, phencyclidine; hallucinogens; and cannabis. It also includes a classification of polysubstance dependence for those individuals who use at least three categories of psychoactive substances, but where no single drug predominates. *Psychoactive Substance Abuse* refers to continued use despite experiencing social, occupational, psychological, or physical problems; recurrent use in situations in which use is physically hazardous, such as driving while intoxicated; and a minimal duration of disturbance of at least one month. *Dependence* refers to the existence of at least three of nine symptoms including loss of control, negative impact on social functioning, continued use despite adverse consequences, and development of tolerance and withdrawal symptoms. In essence, substance dependence refers to compulsive use of a chemical, loss of control over it, and continued use despite adverse consequences. It may vary in severity from mild to severe.

Any psychoactive substance that produces a state of intoxication is liable to be abused and can affect parenting behavior. A knowledge of the distinctive effects of the different types of drugs on a person's thinking and behavior is crucial to the assessment process. The most useful classification of psychoactive drugs is based on their effect on the central nervous system (Carroll 1985) as follows:

Central nervous system depressants—drugs that slow down, reduce the function of, or sedate the excitable brain tissues. Included in this category are: alcoholic beverages, barbiturate and nonbarbiturate sedative-hypnotics (sleeping medications); benzodiazapines (minor tranquilizers such as Librium, Valium, Dalmane, and Serax); anesthetics; volatile solvents (such as toluene); and low doses of cannabinoids (such as marijuana and hashish).

The sedative impact of these chemicals on the brain alters the person's judgment and behavior. Thus, a parent may be slow to react to a child's playing with matches. The individual using these substances also experiences increased agitation and excitability when coming off these chemicals—a feeling commonly known as a hangover. In such a state parents may overreact to a child's crying, for example, and lash out physically without fully appreciating the harmful consequences of their behavior.

Central nervous system stimulants—drugs that increase or speed up the function of excitable brain tissues. Included in this category are amphetamines, cocaine, caffeine, and nicotine. Large doses of such stimulants as amphetamines and cocaine can produce acute delirium and psychosis. The psychotic symptoms can be at times difficult to distinguish from schizophrenia and may include hallucinations, paranoia, and hypersexuality. Amphetamines and more potent forms of cocaine such as "freebase" or "crack" have been noted to contribute to violent behavior.

Narcotics or opiates—drugs that decrease pain by binding to specific receptors in certain brain areas. This category includes opium and its derivatives such as morphine, heroin, codeine, and paragoric, as well as synthetic drugs such as methadone (Dolophine), Demerol, Darvon, Prinadol, Lomotil, and Talwin. Opiates generally tend to have a sedative and tranquilizing effect. However, unlike the users of sedative substances, narcotic users do not usually experience poor motor coordination or loss of consciousness. The opiate-using parent is likely to experience a state of stuporous inactivity and to dwell on daydreaming fantasies and thus be unable to respond to the needs of a child. Due to the physical agitation related to withdrawal and the psychological panic related to anticipation of withdrawal symptoms, violence may occur during drug-seeking behavior or opiate withdrawal.

Psychodelics/hallucinogens—drugs that produce gross distortions of thoughts and sensory processes, thereby inducing a psychosislike state, often with visual hallucinations. Included in this category are the "alphabet drugs" such as LSD, PCP, DOM or STP, mescaline, psilocybin, and large doses of cannabinoids. These drugs may lead to violence due to anxiety and misperception of reality. This is particularly true for users of PCP (angel dust), who frequently experience distorted body image, depersonalization, depression, and hostility.

Various combinations of drugs, such as heroin and cocaine—commonly referred to as speedball; cocaine and alcohol; and others, are frequently used either to counteract the side effects of any one drug or to increase the impact of the drugs. Such polydrug abuse appears to be on the increase and is more likely to be seen among younger parents.

Characteristics of Drug and Alcohol Abusers

Substance abuse, like child abuse, tends to run in families. But no single factor has been identified that accounts for why some people become substance abusers and others do not. Among the possible causes of substance abuse are: biochemical and genetic factors; familial factors; environmental and cultural factors; and personality factors. For example, research studies point to a genetic factor in the intergenerational transmission of alcoholism, especially in males, and to the importance of biochemical factors in narcotic abuse. The abuse of drugs and alcohol has been linked to a paucity of alternatives for a meaningful life, particularly in urban ghettos, and to the influence of peer group and the social acceptance—even cultural idealization—of drugs and alcohol. Studies of female substance abusers, in particular those in lower socioeconomic classes, show a high correlation between substance abuse in women and that of their husbands or boyfriends, indicating the likelihood of women's emotional as well as economic dependence on men as a factor in substance abuse (Straussner 1985). Studies of the backgrounds of alcoholics and opiate addicts in treatment found that they were more likely to experience early separation from one or both parents and tended to receive inadequate care during childhood (Black and Mayer 1980).

No single personality type has been found to predominate among substance abusers. Moreover, it is difficult to get an accurate picture of a substance abuser's baseline state of mental health while he or she continues to use drugs, since symptoms may arise secondarily from the drug use itself. Thus, the effects of alcohol or drugs may be misperceived as symptoms of psychopathology (Levinson and Straussner 1978). Nonetheless, clinicians have related substance abuse to a number of personality and developmental factors.

The abuse of both drugs and alcohol has been viewed as an attempt to diminish anxieties about self-assertion and to obliterate unacceptable feelings of anger and hostility that may, however, be released during intoxication (Kaufman 1985). Some people may turn to alcohol and drugs in an attempt to cope with unacceptable sexual impulses. These substances may also be used to provide a "sense of internal homeostasis which substitutes for the basic lack of a sense of integration of self" (Kaufman 1985, 14).

Both drug and alcohol abusers tend to rely excessively on such defense mechanisms as regression, denial, introjection, projection, and rationalization. Conscious lying as well as minimization of problems are common ways of escaping the consequences of their actions. Kaufman (1985) viewed alcohol and drug abusers as highly impulsive, with low frustration tolerance and an inability to endure anxiety or tension. Their strong dependency needs are usually frustrated, leading to depression and despair as well as rage and fantasies of revenge.

Many substance abusers experience marked mood swings. Although most such mood swings are not necessarily indicative of mood cycle disease, some people do begin to abuse drugs or alcohol in order to "medicate" preexisting emotional disorders such as affective, anxiety, or somatoform disorders. Personality disorders such as borderline, narcissistic, or antisocial personality (Waldinger 1986), as well as psychosis (Soika 1983) may underlie substance abuse among some maltreating parents.

Since no single theory or personality characteristic is sufficient to explain why someone abuses alcohol and/or drugs, it may be best to view substance abuse as a multivariate syndrome in which multiple patterns of dysfunctional substance abuse occur in various types of people with multiple prognoses requiring a variety of interventions (Pattison and Kaufman 1982).

The Relationship Between Drugs and Alcohol Abuse and Child Maltreatment

Alcohol and drug abuse have been consistently associated with child abuse and neglect. In addition, there is a very high correlation between alcoholism and incest (Tormes 1968; Barnard 1984). Substance abuse seems to interact with other factors such as unemployment, poverty, and personality characteristics, predisposing individuals toward domestic violence in general and child abuse in particular (Black and Mayer 1980).

Drinking is estimated to be involved in 38 percent of cases of physical child abuse (U.S. Department of Health and Human Services 1984), and both drugs and alcohol have been clearly associated with child neglect. A recent national survey of thirty-six hospitals around the country, reported by the *New York Times* (September 6, 1988), found that on average 11 percent of pregnant women were using illegal drugs; cocaine was especially harmful to the developing fetus. It has been estimated (Carr 1975) that in New York City alone there were ninety-three thousand children whose mothers were addicted to illegal opiates and twenty-two thousand children whose mothers were in methadone maintenance programs. There are no published estimates on the number of children in households where the father or both parents are substance abusers (Deren 1986). However, it should be noted that both alcohol and opiate abuse are far more common among men than women.

Not all substance abusers are child abusers, however. Child abuse was found most likely to occur in families in which children were cared for by an alcohol- or opiate-addicted mother, families in which there was violence between the parents, and families with lower financial status and poorer living conditions (Black and Mayer 1980).

It is helpful to differentiate between maltreating parents who are primarily opiate as opposed to alcohol abusers. Since opiate use without prescription is illegal, opiate abusers have been viewed as more likely to have antisocial personality with poor ego and superego development (Tooman 1977). They tend to be younger than alcoholics and frequently began using opiates during their late teens before completing their education and functioning as self-supporting adults. They are more likely to be members of minority groups. Since the time and effort necessary to obtain the drug and to pay for the addiction are considerable, the life-style associated with opiate addiction is highly unstructured and generally characterized by poverty and illegal activity (Black and Mayer 1980). Numerous live-in partners, prostitution, and incarcerations are common. Pregnant women dependent on opiates are likely to suffer anemia, heart disease, diabetes, pneumonia, or hepatitis. They are also likely to experience complications during pregnancy and childbirth, including spontaneous abortions, premature births, stillbirths, and breech deliveries (U.S. Department of Health and Human Services 1983). The following case illustrates some of these issues.

Eleven-year-old June and her eight-year-old brother Ramon were placed in a foster home by protective service workers who found evidence of physical abuse of June by her heroin- and crack-abusing father. The children's father, Mr. C., a thirty-year-old Hispanic man, had lived in and out of the house for the last eight years. A high school dropout from an inner-city public school, he had a sporadic work history for most of his adult life and supported himself by selling drugs. Mr. C had been arrested four times and spent several years in prison for possession and sale of narcotics and related charges. During the last year, whenever he was home, he would not allow the children out of his sight and would lock them in the apartment. While his behavior appeared paranoid, he apparently feared that the children might reveal his whereabouts to other drug dealers to whom he owed money or tell someone he was dealing drugs, since he was currently on parole. June was severely beaten when she tried to sneak out of the house while her father was negotiating a drug sale in another room. Protective service workers were called by the maternal grandmother, who lived in the neighborhood and was concerned when she didn't see the children for a couple of days. The children's twenty-eight-year-old mother was in a hospital due to complications following the stillbirth of a son. She had a history of three miscarriages in five years. Although she was assessed as a basically concerned and caring mother, she seemed immature for her age and afraid of her husband, on whom she was financially and emotionally dependent. She tended to use drugs sporadically —usually combining small doses of heroin with cocaine. Her use of drugs appeared to be related to her need to "please my man" and hold onto the relationship with her husband. When her husband needed money for drugs she would resort to prostitution. When he wasn't around she was frequently able to stop her drug use.

Unlike the use of narcotics, the use and even the abuse of alcohol is legal. Consequently, the life-styles and ethnic backgrounds of alcohol-abusing parents vary widely, reflecting the population at large. Addiction to alcohol usually develops slowly and tends to interfere with a person's functioning after adult independence has been achieved (Black and Mayer 1980). Family life with an alcoholic parent is more structured than with an opiate-addicted parent, but is more likely to be characterized by inconsistency in discipline and attention. Role reversal, in which children assume parental roles and responsibilities (Straussner et al. 1979), as well as violence between the parents, serious illnesses, and various accidents are common occurrences.

Physical abuse of children is more common among alcoholic than narcotic-addicted parents. It is most likely to be committed by alcohol-intoxicated fathers or stepfathers. Children with two alcoholic parents have been found to have the greatest incidence of both abuse and neglect (Peters 1986).

Physical abuse of children has also been linked to the use of cocaine and crack and to narcotic abuse even though, as indicated earlier, narcotic intoxication tends to inhibit violent behavior. Frequently, the heroin addict and the methadone user will take other drugs such as alcohol or cocaine in order to enhance the effect of these drugs. It is believed that the majority of maltreating parents who are opiate abusers fall into this category (Tooman 1977). Little is known regarding physically abusive parents who abuse non-narcotic drugs such as LSD, amphetamines, barbiturates, or minor tranquilizers.

The most common form of child maltreatment by substance-abusing parents is child neglect (Black and Mayer 1980). Child neglect among substance-abusing parents can range from general lack of supervision to "total inattention to such basic needs of children as food and clothing" (U.S. Department of Health and Human Services 1978, 59). Narcotic- and alcohol-abusing mothers are usually unable to care for themselves, much less for a young child. Moreover, since many of them grew up in substance-abusing homes, they frequently lack appropriate parental role models and basic knowledge regarding child care skills.

There are other types of child maltreatment that are unique to families in which the parents abuse alcohol or drugs. These may involve the ingestion of drugs or alcohol by infants or children, resulting from parental neglect or nonsupervision (U.S. Department of Health and Human Services 1978) or caused by parents who deliberately administer dangerous or inappropriate substances to their children. Drugs have been used by parents to pacify active or crying children, as in the case of a four-month-old boy who was hospitalized with pneumonia, dehydration, and chronic malnutrition, the results of being fed a mixture of whiskey and water whenever the family became annoyed by his crying (U.S. Department of Health and Human Services 1978). Numerous other cases have been reported in which life-threatening doses of tranquilizers have been forced upon children by their parents (Mofenson 1984). Occasionally drugs are used in a deliberate attempt to poison a child.

Prenatal Impact of Drugs and Alcohol

A unique issue among women who abuse alcohol and/or drugs is the prenatal impact of these substances upon their children. Drug abuse during pregnancy has been categorized as "one of the major causes of child maltreatment . . ." (Tooman 1977, 231). Authorities are taking an increasingly harsh view of damage caused to the fetus and to the newborn by maternal abuse of drugs and alcohol. In many states children born addicted to heroin, illegally obtained methadone, or cocaine are legally viewed as being abused, and hospitals are required to report such cases to local child welfare agencies. Some hospitals are routinely testing every newborn for prenatal exposure to drugs.

Some of the findings associated with maternal abuse of various drugs are:

1. It is estimated that fifty thousand babies born during 1985 suffered from fetal alcohol syndrome and related defects that result from maternal alcohol use during pregnancy (Brody 1986). Prenatal alcohol exposure constitutes the most common teratogenic cause of mental retardation, causes abnormalities of the central nervous system such as microcephaly, poor coordination, irritability in infancy, and hyperactivity in childhood; growth deficiency; and craniofacial abnormalities (Nadel 1985).
2. Chronic opiate use during pregnancy leads to a variety of medical and obstetrical complications including premature labor and post-partum hemorrhage. The use of dirty and shared needles accounts for various systemic infections and the spread of AIDS among female drug users, which is then transmitted to the newborns. Children born to heroin- or methadone-addicted mothers are likely to have low birth weight and abnormally small head circumference.
3. Neonatal narcotic addiction is frequently found in the children of heroin-abusing mothers. Addicted babies usually exhibit withdrawal symptoms within twenty-four to seventy-two hours after delivery. The symptoms, which may persist for several months, typically include tremors, twitching, hyperactivity, high-pitch crying,

frantic sucking, convulsions, respiratory difficulties, and sleep and feeding disorders. Problems such as hyperactivity and impaired attention span appear to continue through early childhood (Deren 1986).

4. Methadone also causes addiction and withdrawal symptoms in infants born to addicted mothers.

5. Maternal use of barbiturates may result in the physical addiction of the newborn, who will experience severe and prolonged withdrawal symptoms similar to those produced by opiates.

6. The use of benzodiazapines, or minor tranquilizers such as Librium, Valium, Dalmane, and Serax, by pregnant women can produce a drug-dependent infant as well as such birth defects as cleft lip and palate. Withdrawal symptoms such as tremors, irritability, hyperactivity, and poor weight gain may become evident only after discharge from the hospital.

7. The use of amphetamines during pregnancy has been associated with various congenital abnormalities, especially cardiac defects, and there is increasing evidence of fetal and neonatal complications resulting from maternal use of cocaine, including a greater frequency of Sudden Infant Death Syndrome (Finnegan 1985) and premature labor.

The possible impact of birth defects and infant addiction on parental bonding and the resulting child maltreatment must be kept in mind. Likewise, the withdrawal symptoms of newborns of drug-abusing mothers, such as irritability, frequent crying, and difficulty in cuddling (Householder et al. 1982), would present difficulties for the best-equipped mother. For drug-addicted mothers who tend to be unemployed, manifest low self-esteem, anxiety, depression, and inadequate parenting, the task becomes almost impossible (Deren 1986). Moreover, due to withdrawal symptoms, the infant may be kept in the hospital for treatment after the mother's discharge, further interfering with mother-infant bonding. The recent increase in cocaine and crack abuse among pregnant women has lead to the phenomenon of what has been termed "boarder babies"—newborns who cannot be cared for by their mothers and who are unable to be placed and thus continue to live in hospitals for months.

Reporting of Child Maltreatment by Substance-Abuse Agencies

Until August 27, 1986, when President Reagan signed Public Law 99-401 amending the federal confidentiality laws, federal regulations regarding the confidentiality of individuals with alcohol and drug problems were interpreted as taking precedence over state laws mandating the reporting of child abuse and neglect. Consequently, workers in drug and alcohol abuse treatment facilities were prohibited from indicating that a maltreating parent or legal guardian was an active participant in a federally funded drug or alcoholism treatment program. The new amendment removes any restriction on compliance with state laws: all alcohol and drug abuse treatment programs must comply with the provisions of the mandatory reporting laws in their states. However, reporting is permitted only when there is an actual danger or harm to the child, and not merely because a parent has abused alcohol or drugs.

Intervention with Substance-Abusing Parents and Their Children

An integrative perspective on intervention with substance-abusing individuals who maltreat their children requires the utilization of a variety of approaches and clinical skills. It also calls upon the worker to assess the appropriateness of existing services and to support agency and social change. Effective intervention with maltreating parents who are substance abusers must take into account two separate problems—substance abuse and child maltreatment. Intervention in situations that may endanger a child cannot wait until the parent is treated for substance abuse, but intervention that is exclusively focused on child maltreatment will not remove the need to treat parental drug and alcohol abuse. To paraphrase a statement made by a speaker during an AA meeting (Wright 1985): If we sober up a child abuser, we may wind up with a sober child abuser.

Due to the prevalence of substance abuse, it is important that questions regarding the use and abuse of substances be asked of *all* adolescents and adults living in families with a maltreated child. Once substance abuse is noted, interventive efforts should include the following:

1. identifying the kinds of substances being abused and the degree of physical and psychological dependence;
2. assessing the degree to which these substances interfere with parenting skills;
3. identifying appropriate community resources that can treat this individual and the other family members affected by the substance abuser—not just the maltreated child;
4. motivating the abuser to obtain appropriate treatment;
5. monitoring progress of treatment;
6. helping the maltreated children and those currently caring for them to understand parental substance abuse and its impact on their ability to parent.

In addition, substance-abusing parents, like all maltreating parents, must be helped to learn appropriate child-care skills and to obtain essential social services. At the same time various efforts must be undertaken to help the children recover from parental maltreatment. Lastly, preventive efforts must be undertaken so that this problem does not continue generation after generation.

Assessment

The first task in dealing with people who abuse drugs or alcohol is to avoid stereotyping them. While some parents may readily admit to being substance abusers, others may not. Thus the worker must ask the "right" questions. Since most people in society do drink and use a variety of medications, the interviewer should start with the assumption that the parents have used some alcohol and other chemicals at some time. The following set of questions can be used to obtain an initial assessment of the extent and effect of such use:

1. How much do you drink a day/week?
2. What do you drink?
3. How old were you when you first started drinking?
4. Are you now drinking more/less than a year ago?

5. Have you ever used _____?/How much?/How often?/When started?/Date of last use?
   a. heroin;
   b. methadone;
   c. cocaine/crack;
   d. marijuana;
   e. sleeping medication (what kind);
   f. tranquilizers (what kind);
   g. other medication/drugs obtained from friends or on the street;
   h. other medication/drugs obtained from a doctor.
6. Have you ever tried to stop drinking/drug use? What happened?
7. Have you ever been in treatment for substance abuse? Where/When/What happened?
8. Have you ever attended AA or NA (or any other self-help group)? How did you feel there?
9. Does/did your mother/father drink too much?
10. Does/did your mother/father use drugs (what kind)?
11. Does your spouse/boyfriend/girlfriend drink a lot/use drugs?
12. Has anyone (spouse/parents/children) ever complained about your use of alcohol/drugs?
13. Do you think that you have a problem with drugs/alcohol?

Answers to the above questions can provide a rough assessment of parental substance abuse. It is to be expected that substance abusers deny and minimize their use of chemicals and the impact of the substance abuse on their lives. Thus it is important to obtain information from other sources, such as other members of the nuclear and extended family or friends, as well as to rely on such clues as the wearing of long sleeves in the summer to cover up needle marks, or the smell of alcohol on the breath—especially early in the day. All maltreating parents whose behavior is highly volatile and unpredictable should be questioned about possible substance abuse.

Workers unsure about their assessment regarding parental substance abuse should refer the parent to an appropriate community agency, such as the local alcoholism council or a substance abuse clinic, to make an assessment. Just as workers may refer a client to a physician for an assessment of a possible physical problem, they need to feel comfortable making referrals for assessment of a substance abuse problem. There is nothing wrong with telling a parent, "I am concerned about your use of (alcohol, drugs, etc.) and want you to go to _____ for an evaluation (or check up)," or "While I believe you when you tell me that you do not have a problem with drugs/alcohol, you must go to _____ for an evaluation before we can make any further plans regarding the children." It is important to realize that once individuals start abusing such substances as alcohol, opiates, or cocaine, they often become addicted to them—that is, they *cannot* just stop using them through will-power alone. They should not be made to feel guilty or condemned for being dependent on a chemical any more than a parent would be condemned for having an uncontrolled medical condition.

It is also important to keep in mind that substance abuse is a "family disease" (Straussner et al. 1979)—that while a maltreating parent may not be the one who abuses chemicals, he may be the spouse or the child of a substance abuser and thus a part of a substance abuse family system, and this may affect his parenting.

Use of Authority to Overcome Denial

Once clients are assessed as being substance abusers, the next step is to make sure that they obtain appropriate treatment. As a rule, substance abusers do not enter treatment voluntarily. Due to the effects of drugs and alcohol on the brain and the extensive use of denial and other defenses by substance abusers, maltreating parents who are substance abusers usually need others to push them into obtaining appropriate help.

Ms. G., a twenty-two-year-old woman of Irish background, was referred to a community-based outpatient alcoholism treatment program by a hospital social worker after she gave birth to an infant with fetal alcohol syndrome. For the past two years, Ms. G. had been living with her alcoholic boyfriend while her three-year-old son from a previous relationship had been living with her mother, her disabled alcoholic father, and her three siblings. Although Ms. G. kept denying that she had an alcohol problem and was angry at the hospital staff for not releasing her baby to her, she agreed to attend the alcoholism treatment program after being told that this would be the only way she could have the infant released to her. Initially highly resistant to treatment, through attendance in psychoeducational groups, individual sessions with a counselor, structured group therapy, and AA meetings she gradually started to examine her drinking and the impact of her behavior on her children, as well as the effect of her father's alcoholism on her. By the time the infant was released to her, Ms. G. was in the beginning process of recovery from alcoholism. Although she resumed drinking three months later following a fight with her boyfriend and stopped attending the alcoholism treatment program, the outreach worker from the clinic convinced her to return to treatment or risk the possibility of having the child removed. Ms. G. returned to the clinic and started the treatment program from the beginning. She completed the structured six-month program without returning to drinking and elected to continue treatment in a weekly women's group run by a social work student at the agency. With the support of the group members she was able to get out of a destructive relationship with her abusive boyfriend and resumed the care of her older son in addition to caring for the infant. She was encouraging her mother, whose own father was an alcoholic, to attend Al-Anon meetings with her.

As exemplified in the above case, recovery from substance abuse is not dependent on whether or not the initial contact with treatment was mandated—as a matter of fact, studies show that individuals who are coerced into treatment may have an even better recovery rate than those who are not (Mark 1988).

Ms. G. needed to be pushed into treatment twice—once by the hospital worker and once by the alcoholism clinic outreach worker. Each time the workers had to resort to using their authority and to threaten her with the only motivating factor available to them: the loss of her child. Had Ms. G. not cared about her child or if she doubted the workers' ability or willingness to follow through with their threat, it's unlikely that she would have followed through with their recommendations.

Such use of authority is an important motivating force for substance abusers of all socioeconomic levels and ethnic backgrounds. It is the basis for the growing number of employee assistance programs as well as drunk-driving programs (King 1986). Its value in pushing substance-abusing parents into obtaining appropriate treatment cannot be underestimated. It is the threat of removal of the child from parental custody that forces many substance abusers to follow through on referrals to treatment, and it can often cause the substance abuser to respond to treatment efforts that have failed in the past.

Treatment Approaches for Substance-Abusing Parents

Workers who identify substance-abusing parents must determine appropriate forms of treatment for these clients. In general, substance-abusing parents need specialized treatment, and workers need to be aware of the various treatment approaches offered for substance abusers in their communities. They must also be familiar with the kind of substance abuse insurance coverage held by the parents and help arrange for essential financial and child care support while a parent is in treatment.

The following treatment approaches are available in most communities:

Detoxification

Detoxification is the first step in the treatment of those physically addicted to opioids, alcohol, barbiturates, other sedative hypnotics, and amphetamines. It is not required for cocaine or crack users. Detoxification is generally carried out on a medical or psychiatric inpatient unit in order to allow for careful monitoring of physical status and to prevent potentially lethal withdrawal reactions.

Although withdrawal from opiates has been given much publicity, it is not life-threatening, as it may be from severe alcohol or barbiturate addiction. It has been compared to "a one-week bout with influenza" (Waldinger 1986, 315). Heroin addicts can be detoxified on an outpatient basis with the help of such chemicals as clondine or decreasing doses of methadone. Whenever possible, inpatient detoxification treatment is recommended, since it increases the likelihood of a comprehensive assessment and a greater acceptance of further inpatient rehabilitation or appropriate outpatient treatment.

Inpatient Rehabilitation Treatment

Detoxification is usually only the beginning of a long and difficult course of recovery. The lives of many substance abusers revolve around the process of obtaining drugs or alcohol; this provides a daily routine as well as a relationship with other substance abusers that must be replaced if the individual is to maintain a drug-free existence. Moreover, when substance abusers give up their chemicals, there is a prolonged period of physiological withdrawal that can last as long as one year, as well as a potentially longer psychological mourning period for the lost substances (Goldberg 1985). Furthermore, since substance abusers often medicate unpleasant feelings such as anxiety or depression, these feelings are likely to surface or worsen when the drug is taken away.

Therefore, short- and long-term inpatient rehabilitation programs and drug-free residential communities are invaluable in helping substance-abusing parents examine, in a generally protective environment, the impact of drugs upon their lives, their parenting skills, their ability to relate to other people, and the necessary changes in their life-style they must undertake if they want to recover from substance abuse. While cocaine and crack users do not require inpatient detoxification, they do require ongoing inpatient or outpatient counseling.

Child welfare workers are frequently reluctant to recommend inpatient treatment to mothers who have primary responsibility for child care. Mothers are afraid of losing custody of their children while they are in treatment; workers are concerned about lack of readily available child care alternatives. However, the long-term consequences of leaving a child in the custody of a parent who does not obtain treatment for substance abuse can be tragic. Although few in number, several treatment facilities exist in which the mother and child can be placed together and which aim to help the mother with her addiction as well as to assist her in providing appropriate care for her child (Tooman 1977).

The Use of Chemical Substitutes: Methadone Maintenance and Antabuse

Methadone maintenance programs alleviate the daily concern about obtaining drugs. They allow narcotic addicts to use individual and group counseling, vocational training, and educational courses in child care, and to improve the overall quality of their lives. The staggering number of AIDS victims among intravenous narcotic users is another important factor in referring maltreating parents to methadone maintenance programs. However, since methadone maintenance programs vary greatly in their provision of supportive and social services, it is important to help maltreating parents examine if their particular program is effective in meeting their particular needs. The fact that a maltreating parent attends a methadone maintenance program does not mean the parent is receiving appropriate help.

A chemical that is sometimes used to help alcoholics is disulfiram, commonly known as Antabuse. It is a medication that blocks the normal oxidation of alcohol so that acetaldehyde, a by-product of alcohol, accumulates in the bloodstream and causes unpleasant and at times even life-threatening symptoms, such as rapid pulse rate and vomiting. This serves as a conscious deterrent to drinking while using Antabuse.

Although short-term use of the above drugs has been supported by many clinicians and researchers, the value of long-term utilization of any one of these chemical substitutes is questionable. They should be viewed as useful adjuncts to other forms of treatment for highly impulsive drug- and alcohol-abusing individuals, but not as total treatment by themselves.

Outpatient Individual Treatment

Outpatient, individual, insight-oriented psychotherapy is not recommended for substance abusers until they are quite secure in their abstinence from chemicals, since the anxiety aroused during treatment may lead to the resumption of alcohol or drug usage. Moreover, due to the impact of the chemicals on the brain and the possibility of "blackouts" (memory loss while intoxicated), individual counseling or therapy with active substance abusers is frequently useless and therefore contraindicated (Levinson and Straussner 1978).

However, if the maltreating parent has stopped using chemicals or is making serious efforts to abstain from drug and alcohol use, ego-supportive treatment can be utilized (Goldstein 1984). Since substance abuse involves substituting a chemical for human contact, a crucial part of an ego-supportive approach is the establishment of a nonthreatening relationship with a caring and consistently reliable individual. The goal of ego-supportive treatment is to enhance the parent's self-esteem and to improve ego functioning.

The view of substance abuse as a disease is invaluable in helping drug and alcohol abusers to alleviate their frequently extreme feelings of guilt and to motivate them to get help. This perspective diminishes the usually negative countertransferential reactions of workers at the same time that it enables parents to examine both their inability to stop abusing drugs and/or alcohol and their maltreatment of children. It may take persistent efforts on the part of the worker to help the clients view their problems in a different way.

Jean, a twenty-seven-year-old woman, was referred to a social worker by the pediatrician caring for her 2½-year-old son. The boy, who tended to be hyperactive, was being seen frequently by the doctor for a variety of illnesses and mild injuries. Jean, who frequently complained to the doctor about her difficulty in coping with the boy, was eager for the referral. Although the doctor did not confront Jean, he did indicate to the social worker that he was concerned about possible child abuse.

During the first two sessions the worker found out that Jean's father, a Scandinavian seaman, died of liver failure related to alcoholism and that for the past two years she had been drinking daily and was using Valium on a regular basis. She felt dissatisfied with her relationship with her husband, who was spending more and more time at work while she was feeling more and more overwhelmed with caring for her son. In order to ascertain both the extent of substance abuse and child abuse, she was asked to describe minutely the last two days from the minute she woke up until she went to sleep. The worker told Jean that such a description would help the worker understand the pressures that Jean was experiencing in her daily life. As her daily routine was discussed and compared to her life a year ago, it became obvious that both Jean's drinking and her inappropriate reactions to her child's behavior had escalated over the last year. While Jean did not think that she had a drinking problem, she was extremely agitated when she described her inability to stop herself from hurting her child whenever he refused to listen to her. The worker assumed the role of an educator, telling Jean that her son's behavior was typical for an active 2-year-old, and that such behavior would be frustrating to most parents. The worker told Jean it was obvious that she was a caring mother who did not want to hurt her son, but when she felt unsupported by her husband, and frustrated by her son, she appeared to lose control.

Using Jean's own description of her daily drinking pattern, the worker explained the impact of alcohol and Valium on the brain and how having these substances in her system would make it impossible for her to control her reactions. Thus she would end up doing things which she did not mean to do. Jean remembered how her father would get drunk, and although he never hit her or her four siblings, he would fight with her mother and then feel extremely remorseful. The worker talked about alcoholism as a disease, described its various symptoms—including feelings of remorse, and how it tends to run in families. While Jean admitted that two of her brothers were alcoholics, she still did not think that she was. The worker told Jean that the only way either of them could be certain of that would be to see what would happen if Jean tried to stop drinking until her next appointment. In the meantime, Jean agreed to call the worker every evening at a set time and tell her if she had been able to stay sober that day.

Jean cut down on her use of Valium and maintained her sobriety for three weeks, but when her son developed an ear infection and became more difficult to manage, Jean went on a drinking binge that scared both her and her husband. At this time, the worker saw Jean together with her husband and once again talked about the disease of alcoholism and how Jean was manifesting many of its symptoms. At the suggestion of the worker, the couple agreed to hire a part-time baby sitter so that Jean did not have to feel guilty whenever she wanted time to herself or over her inability to be a perfect mother (and wife) twenty-four hours a day. Neither Jean nor her husband wanted to consider attending a self-help group, but Jean agreed to think about going to AA if she had another binge. During the next six months Jean continued to drink sporadically, even though her interaction with her son was less problematic. With the encouragement of the social worker, the boy started nursery school and seemed to be doing better.

At the same time Jean's problems with her husband were becoming more overt. Several joint sessions with the couple proved unproductive, as Jean tended to increase her drinking prior to and following these sessions. Jean continued to resist going to AA until, eight months after beginning of therapy, she and her husband got into a physical fight. The worker used Jean's increased anxiety to motivate her to attend AA. Jean began attending a women's AA group and continued in individual therapy. During the next six months Jean had several "slips" or relapses in her sobriety, and her relationship with her husband continued to be problematic. There were no further indications of child maltreatment.

Her individual treatment focused on preventing further relapses by helping her to identify the "triggers" that usually led to her drinking and by helping her to examine her unrealistic expectations of herself as well as of her husband and her son (and, at times, of the worker). Her active involvement in AA and her ability to maintain sobriety in spite of an increasing depression (for which she was prepared by the worker) increased her self-esteem. As her critical superego diminished, her ability to accept her own limitations, as well as those of people around her, increased. Her relationship with her husband began improving and, for the first time, she was able to begin to examine her relationship with her parents and its impact on her present life.

While Jean was resistant to focusing on her drinking, nonetheless she was easy to engage in treatment. This was not true of Louise, a black twenty-two-year-old single mother of two young boys who was reported for child neglect. During the intake interview, Louise was initially extremely hostile and resistant to talking to the worker. She refused to sit down when asked to do so. The worker told Louise that she could understand her feelings of anger at being reported and investigated, but that she assumed that both of them were concerned about making the best plans for the children. The only way she, the worker, could help would be if Louise was willing to talk to her. The worker began asking questions about Louise's current life and relationships. When asked about the use of drugs Louise admitted that she had used heroin in the past and had recently started using crack, which she obtained from a neighbor. She refused to tell the worker how she paid for the drugs and the worker assumed that she was probably prostituting herself. The worker tried to be as nonthreatening and as nonjudgmental as possible; she used universalization and stated that she frequently found that people become seduced by drugs and that in spite of their own desires often do things that they really do not mean to do—that drugs such as heroin and crack make people forget all that they care about, including their loved ones. She wondered if that's what happened to Louise. Louise, who up to this point continued to stand and kept her responses to a minimum, sat down and started talking about what drugs did to her younger brother, who was recently found dead from "some kind of heart condition." Her brother used to live with her and help with caring for the children. The worker acknowledged Louise's loss and the fact that this has been a very traumatic time for her. She wondered if the use of crack was making it easier for her to deal with this loss. Louise did not answer. Slowly she began to cry.

By viewing Louise's problem in a nonpejorative manner and by focusing on her drug use as an addiction over which Louise had minimal control, the worker was able to align herself with Louise and the treatment process was able to commence.

Group Interventions

Group counseling and activities are helpful to many substance abusers. They provide peer interaction, support, and confrontation with the consequences of parental denial, attitudes, and behavior. The value of separate groups for substance-abusing women has been noted by many clinicians (Nichols 1985).

Self-help groups or "twelve-step programs" such as Alcoholics Anonymous (AA), Narcotics Anonymous, Pills Anonymous, and others have proven to be particularly helpful and are available in every community throughout the United States. These groups provide continuously available support and help to replace drinking and drugging companions with a new group of peers with whom the substance abuser can identify. Moreover, self-help groups allow members not only to receive help from others but also to give help to others, thereby enhancing self-esteem. Parents Anonymous, which is based on AA, helps maltreating parents obtain support in dealing with their lack of control, which leads to child abuse. It is a valuable supplement to other self-help programs, and it is common to have a person attend more than one self-help group each week.

All workers in the field of child welfare should attend a few "open" meetings of the various self-help groups—especially AA. At times, it may be helpful to escort a substance-abusing parent to such a meeting or to encourage the parent to call, in the presence of the worker, the main number of the self-help group (available in the phone book) and ask for help.

Intervention with Family Members

Family therapy has been suggested by some as an effective modality for those substance abusers who are already chemically free (Kaufman 1985). Frequently, the spouse or parent of the substance abuser may be more approachable than the maltreating parent. In such cases, efforts should be made to help family members understand the nature of substance abuse and its impact on the family.

It is extremely important to refer family members to self-help groups for families of substance abusers such as AlAnon, PilAnon, Families Anonymous, or NarAnon. These groups help adult family members to examine their own role in the "enabling" behavior (see Levinson and Straussner 1978) that allows for the perpetuation of the problems, and to obtain support from others in the same circumstances. These groups are particularly useful to the parents and wives of alcohol or drug abusers. Adolescent children of alcohol- and narcotic-abusing parents may benefit from such self-help groups as Alateen and Narateen. COA (Children of Alcoholics) groups have been found to be extremely helpful for mature adolescents and adult children of alcoholics and are proliferating rapidly throughout the country.

Social Supports

As indicated earlier, substance-abusing parents who maltreat their children are more likely to be single women and those couples who were experiencing lower financial status and poorer living conditions. Thus, the provision of financial and social supports—including adequate housing and vocational rehabilitation programs—must be an essential aspect of helping this population. According to Black and Mayer (1980, 111), "the provision of social and economic supports during childrearing may be more effective over the relative short time than therapy" in healing maltreating parents and their children.

Intervention with Maltreated Children

The nature of intervention with maltreated children of substance-abusing parents depends on the nature of the maltreatment and the age of the child. Children born addicted must first obtain appropriate medical treatment. Once the child is medically ready for discharge, the decision then has to be made if the child should go to the parent, to a relative, or into placement. Although some parents are better able to cope with such a child than others, as a general rule "there is a real danger of continued maltreatment if the infant is put under the direct care of addicted parents who have not been truly rehabilitated" (Tooman 1977).

Studies of children of drug-abusing parents indicate that one of the most common placements for children is with the maternal grandmother (Deren 1986). Substance-abusing parents, however, frequently come from homes where there has been physical and sexual abuse as well as substance abuse. Therefore, children placed in surrogate care of their grandmothers, as well as other family members, may also be at risk for abuse and neglect (Deren 1986) and should be monitored closely.

Foster care placement of an addicted infant usually follows routine procedure as long as the child has no serious medical problems after detoxification (Tooman 1977). Perhaps because alcohol, unlike heroin, is a socially approved drug, alcoholic parents are frequently less stigmatized than drug abusers, and mandatory separation of infants from their alcoholic parents is rare. Without appropriate treatment, however, children of alcoholics are "no less at risk than those of drug addicts" (U.S. Department of Health and Human Services 1978, 65).

The subtle effects of substance abuse withdrawal may continue long after the infant is discharged from the hospital. The provision of ongoing medical supervision and such services as visiting nurses who are familiar with substance abuse, as well as supportive counseling to the caregivers, are crucial whether the child is in placement or at home. Educating the caregivers regarding the possible impact of substance abuse on the child is essential to prevent additional child abuse by frustrated caregivers. Helping the caregivers understand the nature of the parents' substance abuse also enables them to be more sensitive to and tolerant of these parents—ultimately benefiting the welfare of the children.

The impact of alcoholism on the family has terrifying intergenerational repercussions: children of alcoholics are likely to become alcoholics. Moreover, the daughters of alcoholics are likely to marry alcoholics (Straussner 1985; Peters 1986). Intergenerational repercussions also exist for families with parental opiate addiction: children of narcotic addicts are more likely to abuse drugs and/or alcohol as shown in a study group of teenagers (Sowder and Burt 1980). Thus intervention with school-aged and adolescent children of substance abusers in maltreated families must focus not only on the physical and emotional effects of the maltreatment, but also on helping the child recognize and understand parental and transgenerational substance abuse. School-based programs, such as Student Assistance Programs (Morehouse 1979; Griffin and Svendsen 1986), are invaluable in identifying children of substance-abusing parents who may otherwise be overlooked. Extensive literature written directly for children and adolescents can be obtained from AlAnon and NarAnon and is extremely valuable in helping children begin to understand what has happened to them and potentially to prevent the pattern from repeating itself in the next generation.

Intervention in and Collaboration with the Community

There is a crucial need both for closer coordination between substance abuse and child abuse agencies and for greater understanding of the dynamics involved in each problem population. While alcoholism and drug counselors focus on the parent's substance abuse problem, they fail to deal with existing child care problems; meanwhile, child welfare workers are separating abused youngsters from their homes without motivating substance-abusing parents into treatment (Hindman 1979).

One possible approach to increasing interagency communication would be to have counselors from local substance abuse agencies provide inservice education to child welfare workers. Such training would include information about the nature of substance abuse, its treatability, and the services available in the community. Similarly, child welfare workers could provide the same function for local substance abuse treatment programs. Drug and alcohol treatment programs are crucial settings where parents can be identified (Deren 1986). Substance abuse workers need to learn how to identify child abuse problems and to become knowledgeable about referral resources and the legal issues involved in making referrals. They also need help in analyzing their personal attitudes toward child abusers. The establishment of local task forces comprised of the clients and service providers of both substance abuse and child maltreatment programs would improve communication as well as allow for the formulation of appropriate community-wide intervention strategies. Community intervention cannot be restricted to those already involved in helping substance abusers or to child welfare workers. Hospital and prenatal clinics, domestic violence agencies, and schools as well as the judicial system must become more aware of this doubly troubled population.

Conclusion

This chapter has reviewed the relationship between substance abuse and child maltreatment, described the nature of drug and alcohol abuse, and discussed a practice approach to maltreating parents who are substance abusers. The problem is multidimensional. Appropriate response must include intervention with individuals, family members, and the community at large, and must utilize a range of coordinated interventions.

References

American Psychiatric Association. 1987. *Diagnostic and statistical manual of mental disorders,* 3d rev. ed. Washington, D.C.: APA.

Barnard, C. P. 1984. Alcoholism and incest. *Focus on Family and Chemical Dependency* 7 (1): 27–29.

Black, R., and J. Mayer. 1980. Parents with special problems: Alcoholism and opiate addictions. In *The battered child,* ed. C. H. Kempe and R. Helfer. Chicago: University of Chicago Press.

Brody, J. E. 1986. Personal health. *New York Times,* January 15.

Carr, J. N. 1975. Drug patterns among drug-addicted mothers: Incidents, variance in use and effects on children. *Pediatric Annals* 4: 66–77.

Carroll, C. R. 1985. *Drugs in modern society.* Dubuque, Iowa: W. C. Brown.

Deren S. 1986. The children of substance abusers: A review of the literature. *Journal of Substance Abuse Treatment* 3: 77–94.

Finnegan, L. P. 1985. Focus on illicit drugs. *U.S. Journal of Drug and Alcohol Dependence* 9 (6): 9.

Goldberg, M. 1985. Loss and grief: Major dynamics in the treatment of alcoholism. In *Psychosocial issues in the treatment of alcoholism,* ed. D. Cook, S. L. A. Straussner, and C. Fewell. New York: Haworth Press.

Goldstein, E. 1984. *Ego psychology and social work treatment.* New York: Free Press.

Griffin, T., and R. Svendsen. 1986. *Student assistance program.* Minneapolis: Hazelden.

Hindman, M. 1979. Family violence: An overview. *Alcohol Health and Research World* 4 (1): 2–11.

Householder, J., R. Hatcher, W. Burns, and I. Chasnoff. 1982. Infants born to narcotic addicted mothers. *Psychological Bulletin* 92: 453–68.

Kaufman, E. 1985. *Substance abuse and family therapy.* New York: Grune and Stratton.

King, B. 1986. Decision making in the intervention process. *Alcoholism Treatment Quarterly* 3 (3): 5–22.

Levinson, V., and S. L. A. Straussner. 1978. Social workers as enablers in the treatment of alcoholics. *Social Casework* 59 (1): 14–20.

Mark, F. 1988. Does coercion work? The role of referral source in motivating alcoholics in treatment. *Alcoholism Treatment Quarterly* 5 (3).

Mayer, J., and R. Black. 1977. Child abuse and neglect in families with an alcohol or opiate addicted parent. *Child Abuse and Neglect* 1: 85–98.

Mofenson, H. C. 1984. The chemically maltreated child. *New York Pediatrician* 2: 9.

Morehouse, E. R. 1979. Working in the schools with children of alcoholic parents. *Health and Social Work* 4 (4): 144–62.

Nadel, M. 1985. Offspring with fetal alcohol effects: Identification and intervention. In *Psychosocial issues in the treatment of alcoholism*, ed. D. Cook, S. L. A. Straussner, and C. Fewell. New York: Haworth Press.

Nichols, M. 1985. Theoretical concerns in the clinical treatment of substance abusing women: A feminist analysis. In *Psychosocial issues in the treatment of alcoholism*, ed. D. Cook, S. L. A. Straussner, and C. Fewell. New York: Haworth Press.

Pattison, E. M., and E. Kaufman. 1982. Alcoholism syndrome, definition and models. In *Encyclopedia handbook of alcoholism*, ed. E. M. Pattison and E. Kaufman. New York: Gardner Press.

Peters, K. K. 1986. Child abuse and neglect: The alcoholic parent. In *Child abuse and neglect*, ed. R. Cohen, E. McCabe, and M. Weiss. Albany: N.Y. State Dept. of Social Services, Office of Projects Development.

Soika, S. H. 1983. Mental illness and alcoholism: Implications for treatment. In *Social work treatment of alcohol problems*, ed. D. Cook, C. Fewell, and J. Riolo. New Brunswick, N.J.: Rutgers Center of Alcohol Studies.

Sowder, B., and M. Burt. 1980. *Children of heroin addicts: An assessment of health, learning, behavioral and adjustment problems*. New York: Praeger.

Straussner, S. L. A. 1985. Alcoholism in women: Current knowledge and implications for treatment. In *Psychosocial issues in the treatment of alcoholism*, ed. D. Cook, S. L. A. Straussner, and C. Fewell. New York: Haworth Press.

Straussner, S. L. A., C. Kitman, J. H. Straussner, and E. Demos. 1980. The alcoholic housewife: A psychosocial analysis. *Focus on Women* 1 (1): 15–32.

Straussner, S. L. A., D. Weinstein, and R. Hernandez. 1979. Effects of alcoholism on the family system. *Health and Social Work* 4 (4): 111–27.

Tooman, P. 1977. Disposition and planning long term follow-up of the infant after release from hospital. In *Drug abuse in pregnancy and neonatal effects*, ed. J. L. Rementeria. St. Louis: C. V. Mosby.

Tormes, Y. M. 1968. *Child victims of incest*. Denver: American Humane Association.

U.S. Department of Health and Human Services. 1983. *Opiates*. National Institute on Drug Abuse, Pub. No. 83-1308. Washington, D.C.: U.S. Government Printing Office.

U.S. Department of Health and Human Services. 1984. *Fifth special report to the U.S. Congress on alcohol and health from the secretary of health and human services*. Washington, D.C.: U.S. Government Printing Office.

U.S. Department of Health and Human Services. National Center on Child Abuse and Neglect. U.S. Children's Bureau. 1978. *Substance abuse and child abuse and neglect*. Washington, D.C.: U.S. Government Printing Office.

Waldinger, R. J. 1986. *Fundamentals of psychiatry*. Washington, D.C.: American Psychiatric Press.

Wright, J. 1985. Domestic violence and substance abuse: A cooperative approach toward working with dually affected families. In *Social work practice with clients who have alcohol problems,* ed. E. Freeman. Springfield, Ill.: Charles C. Thomas.

9

Child Maltreatment and the Court

Bonnie Kamen, M.S.W., and
Betty Gewirtz, M.S.W.

Introduction

While only 20 percent of all reported cases of child maltreatment actually result in court involvement (Mayhall and Norgard 1983, 220), both the potential and actual presence of the court exerts a profound impact on families where there is abuse and neglect. Social workers may be called upon to participate at any point in the court process. At intake a child welfare worker might be required to document reasons for filing a petition on why a child was removed from the home on an emergency basis. At fact-finding meetings child protective workers are routinely called on to make available material substantiating the allegations being made. Social workers may be asked to evaluate families formally for the court and may be used to provide expert testimony. They may provide a significant amount of the treatment services for the family. Thus professional roles and practices will differ somewhat depending on where the social worker enters the case and whom the social worker represents.

This chapter will discuss some of the principles underlying court involvement and the various stages of the legal process in child maltreatment cases. Then it will discuss social work role conflict and suggest ways of maintaining role clarity. It will describe a variety of social work roles and the practice principles that stem from them and will conclude by addressing special considerations in child abuse and neglect cases when there is court involvement.

Principles Underlying Court Involvement

When the juvenile or family court was established, it adopted the common law doctrine of *parens patriae*—"the sovereign's ultimate responsibility to guard the interests of children and others who lacked legal capacity" (Mnookin 1973, 603). While the court assumed the authority to intervene in family life, superceding parental control, it did so sparingly. When the concept of representation for children in child protective proceedings emerged, it reflected a formal acknowledgement that the interest of the state, the child, the parents, and the child welfare agency might be different and might lead to conflict. As many states passed legislation mandating legal counsel for neglected and abused children, lawyers assumed a prominent position. Social workers, who had long been central figures in child protective proceedings, moved into more peripheral and subordinate roles. The task of clarifying roles and functions among different professions is an ongoing struggle.

In terms of child maltreatment, the values and standards of lawyers and social workers appear to differ along two dimensions: definitional criteria for abuse and neglect, and the nature of intervention. There are many possible areas of conflict in this complex issue with blurring and difficult boundaries. The law recommends that grounds for coercive intervention be specific, reserved for situations of actual or imminent serious harm, and be of substantial benefit to the child. Social workers traditionally have much more broadly defined what behavior should constitute the maltreatment of a child and justifies coercive intervention for the child's protection. Also, social workers generally have a different view than lawyers of what optimal treatment for maltreatment cases should entail.

There are three important concepts that are basic to understanding some of the controversies involved in maltreatment cases: (1) family autonomy; (2) the best interests of the child; and (3) the least detrimental alternative. Family autonomy refers to the rights of parents to raise their children as they deem appropriate, without intrusion of the state. This concept assumes that the child's best interests generally are most adequately provided for within the context of strong family ties. If the priority of the law is to maintain family integrity, then coercive intervention would require careful limiting and should, even when necessary, be directed toward restoring and rehabilitating the family unit (Mayhall and Norgard 1983, 266; Goldstein, Freud, and Solnit 1979, 4–12).

The "best interests test," however, subordinates family autonomy when the state establishes that there is child abuse or neglect. In utilizing this test, the court compares the parental environment with existing alternatives and makes a judgment regarding which situation is more likely to promote the child's well-being (*Univerisity of Chicago Law Review* 1968, 480).

In contrast to the "best interests test," the concept of the least detrimental alternative suggests that the court weigh its choices for child care on the basis of a realistic appraisal of existing resources rather than in the abstract with little direct knowledge of the specific alternative environments available (Mayhall and Norgard 1983, 268; Goldstein, Freud, and Solnit 1973, 53–64; Mnookin 1973, 615).

In sum, the fact that children need protection under certain circumstances is a commonly held ethic. Specifying when, what, and how intervention is to occur, however, remains controversial. An awareness of the philosophical issues and practical dilemmas embedded in this controversy can help the social worker in assessment, decision making, and planning and implementing intervention.

Stages of the Legal Process

Intake

The child protective system goes into operation in response to child maltreatment when a report of suspected neglect or abuse is made to an officially designated public or private agency through any one of a variety of sources. Such agencies and their processes vary from state to state and may include local police, social service agencies, the juvenile or family court, or an authorized public or private child protective service. The investigative agency, in most localities a legally mandated child protective service, retains a large measure of discretion in determining whether a reported case requires simple screening out, full exploration, court intervention, and/or a range of family services. Research has indicated that initial interventions in response to complaints of child neglect or abuse are shaped more by the practices of the particular agency first contacted than by the severity of the maltreatment itself or other case characteristics. For example, it was found that the police removed children on an emergency basis more frequently than did child protective service workers (Miller et al. 1982).

In situations in which the screening agency places the child on an emergency basis, a court hearing must be held within a specified period of time to determine whether the child's removal should be sustained. When temporary placement is contested by the parents, another hearing may take place in which the burden of proof is on the agency to show why the child should remain out of the home.

It appears from all available findings that it is largely the most severe maltreatment cases within those families hardest to engage in interventive efforts that come to the court's attention (Giovannoni and Becerra 1979, 230). Thus court involvement may well be the end point in a successive filtering process representing the last remaining alternative when all other viable solutions have been exhausted. Social workers currently providing assessment and treatment services to maltreated children and their families report that these families typically have a history of intermittent, crisis-oriented contact with multiple helping agencies. In a major study of maltreated children and their families, it was found that families viewed as "cooperative," despite the severity of the maltreatment, tended to remain solely within the child welfare services network rather than being referred for court actions (Giovannoni and Becerra 1979).

The following brief clinical vignettes will compare severely abusive parents who are cooperative with those who are uncooperative.

The uncooperative family consistently denies the allegations of abuse, keeps the child away from authorities, does not follow through on recommendations, and continues the abusive behavior. The Williams family was designated as uncooperative by child welfare authorities. When the school officials informed the parents that they were reporting them to Special Services for Children, the parents sent the abused child to a relative. When child welfare workers asked to see the child, the parents sent them on a "wild goose chase." Because of the uncooperative behavior of the parents, the workers referred them for court action. The uncooperative behavior of the parents was one important factor in the assessment that determined the family was not amenable to treatment.

The Lewis family had seriously abused their child. When child welfare authorities visited the family, the parents allowed the child to be interviewed. The parents were remorseful about their abusive behavior and were willing to cooperate with the child welfare workers. This case stayed within the jurisdiction of the child protective agency. The parents' admission of abuse was one of the factors in the assessment of family dynamics that led the case to remain in the child protective agency.

Fact Finding

The next stage in the court process is the fact-finding hearing, during which the judge will decide if the allegation(s) in the petition have been sufficiently proven. The standard of proof required in the neglect and abuse proceedings can be either "clear and convincing" or "a preponderance of the evidence." When the parents challenge the allegation(s) against them, evidence may be presented by all parties in the dispute. Witnesses will be called on to provide testimony. If the parents admit to the allegation(s) or if the judge decides that the allegation(s) have been substantiated, a finding of neglect or abuse is made. Some cases that originate as abuse may be adjusted down to neglect; others, despite containing both neglect and abuse allegations, will result in a finding of neglect only. If the allegation(s) are not founded, the case is dismissed. For a finding of neglect and/or abuse to be made, however, not all the allegations contained in the petition must be proven.

It is during the fact-finding stage that the court's jurisdiction over the case is formally established. Once child neglect and/or abuse is adjudicated, the court must proceed to determine the appropriate action to be taken. To assist the court in this task various agencies (probation, child protective services, mental health units, and so on) may be ordered to provide investigative and evaluative reports. These reports usually contain recommendations that the court considers fully or in part when making a disposition.

Disposition

At the dispositional stage, typically a separate hearing, the court reviews the material submitted and endorses a specific interventive plan (disposition). The following plans may be ordered by the court:

1. A case may be adjourned in contemplation of dismissal (ACD), remaining active for up to one year. The family may be ordered or recommended to cooperate with child protective or other treatment services, and can be immediately brought back to court if new incidents of mistreatment arise. If there are no new occurrences, the case may be dismissed automatically when the ACD period expires.

The Dalton family received an adjournment for one year and was monitored by the public child protective agency. The family was also referred to a social agency for treatment. The practitioner used the leverage of the court in interventions by explicitly informing the parents of the worker's phone contacts with the protective services worker at regular intervals. For example:

Worker: The court is still very concerned about your situation. The child welfare worker called me last week.

Client: What did she want to know?

Worker: If you are attending sessions every week and how you and your child are getting along. I told her that you are coming regularly and working with me on your problems.

Severely abusive parents often will need to feel that they are being monitored by the authorities in order to control their abusive tendencies. The worker shows empathy as well as use of authority by explaining to the parents that the monitoring is to protect them as well as the child, since abuse can tragically destroy the entire family.

2. Formal supervision by child protective services or another court authorized agency may be ordered. Here the family must cooperate with the agency's treatment plan and the agency must moni-

tor the family situation on a regular basis. Court-ordered supervision implies that the child, despite having been returned to the parent's custody, still requires the court's protection.

3. The child may be remanded to the custody of child welfare authorities (placement in foster care, residential placement or a group home for a specified period of time).

4. When a case involves parental abandonment, lack of cooperation with treatment, and/or sustained failure to provide an adequate home, a proceeding to sever parental rights may be initiated with the goal of freeing the child for adoption.

5. Dispositions can order that the child be placed in the custody of a relative or other interested party.

6. An order of protection may be issued for the purpose of safeguarding the custodial parent and/or child from the actions of another party whom the court deems as potentially dangerous. A very brief clinical vignette will illustrate the type of situation in which a court order might be used. Ms. Franklin lived with a boyfriend who physically abused her and her children. With the threat of losing her children, Ms. Franklin made the boyfriend move out. However, he continued to hang around her house and follow her and the children. When she told him to stop bothering them, he threatened her. With the help of the child protection agency worker, Ms. Franklin took out a court order that prevented the boyfriend from going near her house or following her. The worker from protective services for children spoke to the local police to ensure their cooperation if Ms. Franklin called because of harrassment.

The roles and functions of the key participants will vary according to the stage of the court process. Each stage of this court procedure is guided by a different unifying principle. The fact-finding phase requires the meeting of an evidentiary standard, while the dispositional phase utilizes the "best interests of the child test" in determining a plan that focuses the court's attention on the child.

Role Clarity

Although social work roles and tasks appear straight-forward in theory, their practical implementation is too often confusing and conflictual. The position of social workers as both accountable to and extensions of the legal system in child maltreatment cases may threaten professional autonomy and a sense of competence. Forensic practice confronts the social worker with a range of value dilemmas and role ambiguities. Self-determination conflicts with the coercive aspects of involuntary intervention. Maintaining a nonjudgmental attitude is at variance with social control functions. Confidentiality in the client-worker relationship contrasts sharply with reporting to the court. The inherent tension between the court's familial and legal obligations affects the court process itself and the professionals who are asked to serve it.

In work with maltreated children and their families, role clarification is an ongoing process. Each worker on the case, regardless of the point of entry, needs to ask:

1. For whom am I working—the court, the foster care agency, a mental health clinic?
2. With whom am I working—the child, the foster parents, one or both of the natural parents, or extended family members?
3. Who is working with me—lawyers, foster care workers, child protective service workers, day care workers, school personnel, homemakers, parent aides?

Unique to maltreatment cases is the worker's concurrent involvement with more than one client (either primarily or collaterally) and with multiple service providers. Role clarity derives from a solid understanding of one's place in the overall interactive scheme, the expertise one brings to the task and, just as significantly, the conviction that one's role is meaningful. From this position it becomes possible for colleagues to work together effectively and, equally important, this provides a foundation for future client involvement. Notably, clients entering the court child welfare system experience fragmentation and confusion of their own. The worker who can approach a client with a coherent sense of purpose and without ambivalence is in the best position to begin the engagement process. Conflicts of purpose, function, and conviction inevitably arise when difficult case decisions must be made or lived with.

For example, a child welfare worker might refer a child abuse case to the court. The worker might feel that the child is in danger and should be removed from the home, but the court might not take this action but instead place the family under the supervision of the public child protection agency. The worker might feel troubled by the court's decision but still must follow the court order to the best of his or her ability.

Another example is that a child protective agency worker might be trying to help a psychotic, abusive mother who cares about her young children but is not able to meet their needs. The worker knows that the mother will be upset and hurt by the removal of the children but that she is still too unstable to care for them. In this situation, the worker must act to protect the children but will feel conflicted over the pain that placement will cause the mother. Airing these issues is most constructively achieved in the context of supervisory or collegial relationships that provide support, the opportunity to review and make sense of recent events, and sustained continuity.

Role clarity is best achieved and maintained by remembering that:

1. accountability extends beyond the worker's own agency borders to include the court and child protective services;
2. interagency alliances among professionals and paraprofessionals at different points in the process need to be established and maintained, particularly around critical decision making. For instance, should a child in treatment require placement, interagency collaboration can expedite a successful placement plan.
3. Crisis periods can be expected to disrupt ongoing treatment. Rarely do maltreatment cases progress sequentially. Complications that typically arise require workers to shift practice functions in midstream. For example, a parent's sudden withdrawal from a substance abuse program might necessitate reassessment of the home situation and modification of previously set goals.

Role clarity involves a degree of flexibility oriented around the changing needs of the client and the worker's accountability to the court and child protective agency.

Social Work Roles and Functions

The Child Protective Services Worker

Protective service workers are often the first to come in contact with families about whom child maltreatment reports have been made. The role of the child protective services worker consists of a complex set of responsibilities including investigative, monitoring, and supportive service functions. All tasks related to the performance of these duties center around responding to and/or averting a crisis. The preeminent and compelling concern of child protective services worker must always be assessing whether or not a situation of actual or imminent danger exists.

The Investigation

The investigation protocol will typically include visiting the family's home, making a sight appraisal of the conditions, interviewing all family members, and contacting the person(s) or authority(ies) making the complaint. Formulating a quick assessment, making rapid and well-considered judgments, and taking unilateral action are specific to the initial task. The rules for crisis intervention and an authoritative use of the professional role apply here. If no actual or imminent harm is presented, the child protective service worker's tasks may then shift to more broadly based case planning.

The Case Plan

Case planning in protective services refers to further exploration of the family situation with the objective of formulating and implementing a needs assessment. Continued contacts with family members and significant others, for example, schools and any other agencies to which the family may be known, will provide the worker with a picture of the family's past and current functioning. Of particular importance is exploration of the following areas:

1. prior incidents of maltreatment and their outcomes;
2. previous services offered—when these were provided, by whom, for how long, and how they were utilized;
3. recent changes in the family situation, such as an alteration in the family's composition or household;
4. present situation—identifying information on household members, income and its distribution, health problems, and child care arrangements.

It should be remembered that although the child protective services worker's focus is, by necessity, on the here-and-now, examination of the family's history can enhance the overall viability of the needs assessment by elucidating functional and dysfunctional client behavior patterns, both intrafamilial and environmental. Knowledge of these patterns will enable the worker to predict and manage client responses to protective services intervention and subsequent services offered. Two goals are served here: maximizing client motivation to get help, and discriminating among services to avoid replicating past failures.

In matching clients with appropriate services several points merit consideration:

1. What are the existing resources and their functions?
2. What entitlement programs are available and what are their eligibility requirements?
3. What is the most effective way of sequencing the provision of services? A flood of services can be overwhelming to a family and may be more reflective of the worker's anxiety than the family's needs.
4. What resources can be developed within the family, such as enlisting the help of extended family members to provide child care?

Facilitating the Referral

Particularly important in facilitating the referral is the process of preparing the client for the agency as well as the process of preparing the agency for the client. Pretreatment preparation of the client by the worker should include:

1. clarifying the reason for referral;
2. describing the kinds of services being offered;
3. outlining the intake procedures;
4. concretely arranging for the first appointment if necessary;
5. addressing the client's questions and concerns;
6. discussing the implications of the client's failure to follow through, such as the initiation of court action.

Similarly, all referrals to agencies should be preceded by the worker's making direct contact with the prospective service providers in order to discuss the referral being made, provide identifying data on the case, and obtain information regarding the referral mechanism and intake procedures. A brief clinical vignette will illustrate.

Ms. Thomas and her fifteen-year-old son Duane both requested placement for Duane outside of the home after physical fights between them escalated in violence. The mother had always disciplined Duane by physical force, and now that he had grown, he was hitting her back. The assessment indicated that placement was in order, so the child protective service worker called the placement service of the community family social agency.

The child protective service worker provided the family identifying data, then said, "Duane has no known history of drug or alcohol abuse, violent behavior outside of the home, or any known criminal activity. There is also no direct indication of a serious psychiatric disorder. Rather, our assessment shows that he is a youngster who was never disciplined except by physical force and now has begun to fight back. Therefore, he needs a placement that provides clear rules and regulations but not one where the children are seriously acting out or have serious psychiatric conditions."

This information guided the placement worker to select a residence where the children were predominantly neglected or had minor behavioral problems. The child protective worker then told Ms. Thomas to call the placement service worker directly to request help. The child protective worker said, "I've already contacted the placement worker. Her name is Ms. James and this is her telephone number. I've told her about the problem as you and I agreed and she knows who you are and expects your call."

When to Go to Court

An ever-present concern to child protective service workers is the critical decision of when to initiate court action. Petitioning the court should be considered whenever the worker assesses that the family's situation has moved beyond the control of the protective services agency. Further incidents of maltreatment, for example, or the family's sudden and unplanned withdrawal from services, should suggest to the worker that the authority of the agency has been exceeded. The power of the court is required to effect specific legal action, such as removing a child from the home, or in instances where a child remains at risk, it can be used to order a parent's compliance with treatment.

Case Recording

Remembering that the court's jurisdiction is contingent upon fact finding, workers must be prepared to document their activities, including direct contacts with clients and collaterals. Of particular importance will be the notation of the workers' direct observations. The child protective services attorney will be helpful in placing the client's action within a legal frame and focusing the worker on case material likely to be the most relevant in a court action.

The Foster Care Agency Worker

An abused child can be placed in foster care either through court order or voluntarily by the parents. When a child enters foster care, primary case planning and management shift from child protective services to the foster care agency.

The foster care worker assumes a number of responsibilities including easing the child into the placement, monitoring the care of the child, and planning for the child's permanent living situation. Foster care is always a temporary solution to a crisis of family disruption. The worker plans for a permanent home situation for the child either by reunification with the natural family or through initiating steps to free the child for adoption. The worker will sometimes work with the natural parents and child to promote or preserve the bond between them. A clinical vignette will illustrate this process.

Mrs. Martinez agreed to place her children in foster care after repeatedly abusing them during drinking bouts. She was remorseful and cooperative and joined Alcoholics Anonymous. The foster care worker explained to the children that their mother did care for them but had a drinking problem and was getting help for it. When the mother and children were ready, the worker met with them together in an effort to preserve the familial bond. The worker also met with the foster parents and helped them to see the necessity to support the bond between Mrs. Martinez and her children. The worker helped the foster parents by emphasizing the importance of their role in providing a temporary safe haven for the children while their mother dealt with her problems.

Case Management

The case manager is responsible for interagency collaboration. This function is especially important with maltreating families, who are often receiving services from more than one agency or institution. The case manager centralizes communication among service providers, makes sure each agency knows what the other is doing with the client, and determines if the client needs a referral for further service. The case manager makes sure that there is interagency phone contact and conferences and that the client is not served in fragmented isolation.

The Social Worker as Evaluator for the Court

Prior to court disposition, individuals and families may be ordered to undergo an evaluation at a court-affiliated mental health clinic. Social workers providing assessments to the court work for the court itself and, as an arm of the court, take on a derivative authoritative role. For the client, the helping role of the court-appointed social work evaluator is secondary and indirect. Confidentiality of the client-worker relationship cannot be upheld, nor can the client's right to self-determination be protected. Social workers as court evaluators must clearly identify with the court's unilateral decision-making power and the needs of the client within this legal context.

The social worker doing a legal assessment begins by seeing all significant family members both inside and outside of the household. Family members should be seen individually and together. The social worker assumes an active stance in assessment. From the first contact with the client the worker's role and interview purpose should be clearly communicated. An introductory statement should include: one's name and title, name and purpose of the agency, who referred the client, who else in the family will be seen, who else in the agency the client will see, the layout of the interviewing process, the areas of interest to be explored, how the information will be used, and what questions the client might have.

The evaluation should be interactive as opposed to a question-answer approach. The worker asks about the abuse directly but also wants the client to discuss whatever difficult life situations, personal history, or significant events might have given rise to the abuse. If the client should present gaps, discrepancies, or avoidance around certain issues, the evaluator should express explicit recognition that some issues are difficult to discuss but also assert that it is in the client's interest to be open and honest.

All of the clinical evaluations submitted to the court contain recommendations for court action. Specific and individualized recommendations are more useful than global ones that do not take into account gaps in service delivery or limitations of agencies. The recommendation should be possible to put into action.

Therapeutic Intervention

A child maltreatment case may be voluntarily referred for treatment by a child protective services agency or involuntarily referred for services by court order. The client entering treatment faces a role transition; the client must shift from being a client in the legal sense to becoming a client in a social agency context. The social agency worker must combine empathy and the use of authority with court-referred maltreating parents to a greater degree than with noncourt-referred maltreating parents. Therefore, the court-referred maltreating client remains in a quasi-legal position even as a social service client.

Whether a client enters treatment at the suggestion of a child protective service or is ordered by the courts, a measure of coercion is present. Coercion may be necessary, because there are some maltreating parents who would never come to treatment without the pressure of the court or the child protective agency. The problem that the worker faces with the coerced client is how to combine empathy and authority in interventions to help the parent cooperate in treatment and stop the abuse of the child. The worker's task is to transform an involuntary treatment relationship to one of mutual problem solving.

This is no easy task for even the most experienced of workers. Nevertheless, without being overly optimistic, it can be said that some coerced clients can be helped to stop abusing their children.

How to Begin with the "Coerced Client"

The worker begins with the same process of "getting to know the client" that has been discussed in chapter 3. After the worker has a sense of the client as a person, the worker describes the function of the agency and discusses what is known about the client's problem and the court mandate. The worker then asks the client to talk about the problem. Though the client's attendance at sessions is mandatory, the client's participation in the actual treatment is always voluntary. The client has to choose "to use" the treatment relationship or not. The worker should firmly take the position that the client is expected to fulfill the court mandate, but should also allow the client to express negative feelings and thoughts about it. The worker might say, "As we both know, the court ordered that you come for counseling. This is a requirement that you must fulfill. The court has ordered that you attend, but the court has not required that you tell me that you like attending or that you agree with the court order. Therefore, it would be good for you to be honest about what you think about coming here—whether you are just coming because the court ordered it or whether you have any interest yourself in being here."

In this way, the worker attempts to promote the voluntary participation of the coerced client.

In working with coerced clients the worker must always spell out the consequences of the client's actions. Clients' self-determination must be within the context of the use of authority. For instance, the worker might say, "If you hit your child again, it will be necessary to remove him from the home. If you feel that you cannot control yourselves it would be better for you and for the child that we face this possibility now. It is sometimes necessary for the child to live temporarily away from home." This intervention is suited for severe court-referred cases where the child could be in great danger. The worker attempts to communicate to the parent that there is a choice in having the child live away from home but there is no choice about abusing the child. The worker thereby expresses empathy for the possibility that the parents might not be able to control themselves but also uses authority to limit the abuse.

Reoccurrence of Maltreatment

Reoccurrence of maltreatment in the course of treatment is not uncommon with court-referred clients. The possibility of reporting is of concern to workers and clients from the outset of treatment. In high-risk cases, the worker should clarify as soon as possible the legal obligation to report, the reasons for reporting, and that the client will be advised if reporting is necessary. The worker should view the discussion of reporting with the client as an important intervention that might prevent further child abuse. The worker should also explain that reporting child abuse can save the family from an irreparable tragedy.

In the event that reporting becomes an impending reality, the worker should inform the client directly. Careful clinical judgment is needed to determine whether or not the worker makes his or her individual role in the reporting prominent. In the case of a violent client, for instance, the worker might say that the agency or institution of which she is a representative will be filing the complaint. In most cases, the worker should emphasize that reporting is a legal requirement but also that it serves to protect all family members. A brief clinical vignette will illustrate.

Mrs. Marks was a court-referred abusive parent. In the course of treatment, her child reported to the worker that his mother was drinking alcohol and starting to hit him again. The worker confronted the mother about what the child said and informed her that he'd call her child protection worker at Special Services for Children. The mother said that she did not hurt the child and pleaded with the worker not to call. The worker acknowledged that the child had not yet been hurt but that the worker was calling the protective agency to protect mother and child before the abuse became worse. A home visit and investigation by the child welfare worker confronted the mother and helped motivate her to give up drinking. The child did not have to be removed from the home. In this case, the use of authority was an important part of the treatment plan. The client was a severely abusive parent who could lose control without the help of a monitoring external authority.

Preparing the client that a report is about to be made involves:

1. Reviewing the client's statements made during treatment that point to the need for outside intervention;
2. Restating to the client the agency's and worker's legal responsibility to protect children from harm;
3. Reaffirming the commitment to the treatment process and continued work together;
4. Emphasizing to the family the protective function in reporting of an incident.

In working with severely abusive court-referred parents, the worker should be especially careful never to discuss placement of the child as a punitive action. The possibility of placement needs to be openly discussed with the parent, but the worker should emphasize the protective, helping function of placement. The removal of a child from the home should be undertaken only in severe cases in which the physical well-being or life of the child is endangered. It is precisely in these severe cases that the worker might have to effect placement of a child. The worker's task will be complicated if the parent has been given the sense that placement is a punishment. Empathy and authority work together in intervention when the worker speaks of placement as a realistic possibility or necessity for the protection of the child and the parents.

Mrs. Ortiz was a severely abusive parent referred by the court for treatment. When angry at her children, she'd scream to the worker that she'd teach them a lesson by sending them away. When afraid of the authorities, she'd plead with the worker not to punish her by sending the children away. The worker always intervened by explaining to the mother, time and again, that if the authorities or Mrs. Ortiz decided to send the children away, it would be to help and protect both the children and the mother. Mrs. Ortiz came in one day and told the worker that she must be separated from the children for a time to protect them and herself from murder. She did not say this out of frustration or anger but from serious concern. The worker arranged for immediate referral. A psychiatric interview revealed that Mrs. Ortiz was experiencing delusional homicidal ideation towards the children with a real threat of acting out. The worker's emphasizing the protective aspect of placement and never using it as a punishment enabled Mrs. Ortiz to think of placement when she started to become homicidal.

Client-Worker Traps

Workers may have many attitudinal responses to involuntary clients. They may feel burdened, resentful, and discouraged, or controlled and angered at being told what to do and whom to see, particularly in relation to the court's authority.

With respect to clients, these attitudes can generate problems in the treatment relationship. Client and worker may both feel like victims of an external authority that traps them in an involvement neither wants. Or the worker may envision himself as a magical rescuer who will save the client from the common enemy, the court. In other situations, the worker may identify with the court as an aggressor and attempt to teach the client a punitive lesson. The other side of this is when worker and client fulfill the court mandate that they must meet but neither party works very hard at any change. Lastly, cases providing two treatment providers, such as counselor and parent aide, may result in a "good guy vs. bad guy" scenario. Here the client views one worker as all-good and the other as all-bad. The "good" worker can foster this perception in competition with the other worker or try to gain gratification from the client's positive perception. This last type of pitfall is especially relevant when an abusive parent is monitored by a child protective agency and seen for treatment in a social agency setting. Often, the child welfare worker is viewed as all-bad, the social agency worker as all-good. The client can try to engage the "good" counselor into an aliance against the "bad" child protection worker.

Mrs. Harding hit her son across his body with a bat. She called her social agency worker and told the clinician of the incident in a remorseful tone. The worker stated she'd have to notify the child welfare worker who monitored the client. Mrs. Harding began to tell the worker how she was the only one who ever understood her and the child welfare worker only wanted to hurt her. Mrs. Harding pleaded with the "good" worker not to report her because the child welfare worker could never understand and all the client needed was the good worker to help. The social agency worker stated that she would notify the child welfare worker and the mother became immediately enraged and began cursing the worker. The worker insisted that the child welfare worker was not out to harm the mother and that Mrs. Harding needed protection and help. The mother finally calmed down and agreed the child welfare worker was not "all-bad."

Progress Reports

Under routine circumstances, social workers who treat court-involved clients may be asked to submit reports to the court and/or other agencies concerning a client's treatment. Confidentiality and the therapeutic alliance must be weighed against the obligation to inform accurately. It is typically expected that progress reports will not divulge in depth and detail therapeutic communications. The major interest in progress reports is to know whether or not the client is actively participating in the treatment process. It is important, whenever possible, to review progress reports with clients before they are sent out.

Special Considerations

Evidence

As child protective proceedings become more formal and adversarial, court determinations increasingly rely on data that meet evidentiary standards. In law, evidence constitutes proof of fact. It may be direct, such as the worker's conversation with a client; real, such as bruises on a child; circumstantial, such as the worker's observing signs of drug and alcohol intoxication; or expert opinion presented by a specialist (Landau 1974, 76–77).

Court-related social work practice calls for collecting data that are relevant, admissible, and credible. "Reliable evidence is consistent and stable. Consistent evidence is largely the same even if gathered by different people in the same situation" (Barth and Sullivan 1985, 131). "Validity is less surely established when the measures are intended to indicate something more than is evident at face value . . ." (Barth and Sullivan 1985, 131).

When nonlegal professionals enter the court arena, "second guessing" what the court wants to hear is often an attempt to ameliorate anxiety, defend against potential criticism, and exert control. Addressing issues such as parent-child bonding, parental love, or potential harm may tempt the clinician to overreach professional boundaries. It is important to remember that clinical evidence is not expected to meet the "beyond a reasonable doubt" standard. The clinician need not "defend" the subjective and impressionistic nature of clinical data. With respect to mental health testimony, the Supreme Court has determined that the "clear and convincing" level of proof satisfies due process requirements (Goldstein et al. 1986, 153–57). A mental health practitioner need not prove the unprovable by pretending total objectivity or absolute knowledge.

Testimony

In child protective proceedings, a witness may qualify as material or expert. Usually, child protective services workers testify as material witnesses. Material evidence consists of factual information that substantiates the allegations. Only an expert witness, recognized as a specialist, is permitted to present informed opinion and conjecture in relation to the facts. To qualify as an expert witness a social worker must establish herself as having both credentials and experience in the appropriate area. This will usually entail providing the court with a verbal *curriculum vitae* and a statement regarding the number of similar cases seen.

Being subpoenaed to testify is commonly anxiety-provoking. Preparing for this experience is the most effective means towards mastering this discomfort and performing competently. Preparation includes first and foremost knowing the case facts thoroughly. This does not imply that every detail must be memorized. However, material brought to the court should be organized in such a way that ready reference to particular data is possible. If an error is made or information is missing this should be nondefensively acknowledged. Written notes are permitted but cannot be relied upon while testifying. Testimony cannot be read in speech form.

Testimony, like the written report, attempts to inform, instruct, and convey a point of view. Here again these purposes are best served when testimony is rendered in a nontechnical, descriptive, and reasoned way. Testimony is addressed to the attorney and the judge. The judge may also ask questions independently. It is appropriate to request assistance from either when questions are unclear. The judge will be helpful in addressing confusion that arises regarding aspects of courtroom procedure or can be asked for permission to elaborate on a point about which the attorney has not directly inquired.

Examination and cross-examination are the means through which testimony is elicited. This process is inherently oppositional and, as expert witnesses, workers can expect their testimony to be challenged. Part of preparing to testify, then, is to anticipate what areas of the testimony might be probed and to have available supporting data that strengthen one's point of view. The agency attorney can be helpful in this process.

Not all examination and cross-examination is toward illuminating the case. It is the attorneys' role to cast doubt on the credibility of testimony that could be potentially damaging to their clients. Discrediting strategies might include posing leading questions, insisting on a yes or no response, pushing for absolute statements, and exposing gaps in knowledge of the case.

The following exchange is instructive:

Attorney: Don't you think it's good for the relationship that a mother have contact with her child: (Here the attorney is using a universally accepted psychological theory to lead the worker away from the case specifics to a yes response).
Worker: Yes.
Attorney: But your report recommends that visits be denied. Your report says the child is distant and fearful with his mother. How do you expect them to build a relationship if you're recommending they can't have contact? (Here the lawyer has successfully put the worker off-balance by forcing "self-contradiction").
In response to the same question, the worker might have said:
Worker: This depends on many factors. (Here the worker would have avoided being led into an absolute statement by opening the way for further elaboration).

It should be noted that at times a worker may be subpoenaed but actually not testify. On occasion in family court proceedings a witness will be invited to participate in an informal conference in the judge's chambers. Out-of-court resolutions can be reached through this process and a court disposition made without a hearing.

Conclusion

This chapter has discussed the importance of understanding court procedures; the differences in perception of attorneys, judges, and social workers; and the need to maintain one's own role and perspective when collaborating with other professionals to bring about the best results for the child and family. We have also reviewed the types of interventions that social workers might use in working with maltreating clients involved with the court.

The future of legal and social intervention in child maltreatment cases requires practice studies to determine which interventive strategies are most effective with particular types of maltreatment cases. Longitudinal studies are needed to investigate the large impact of both the legal and social services systems, for example to determine how many delinquent and incorrigible youth presently before the courts actually were once abused and neglected children.

References

Barth, R. P., and R. Sullivan. 1985. Collective competent evidence in behalf of children. *Social Work* 30 (2): 130–36.

Giovannoni, Jeanne M., and Rosina M. Becerra. 1979. *Defining child abuse.* New York: Free Press.

Goldstein, Joseph, Anna Freud, and Albert J. Solnit. 1973. *Beyond the best interests of the child.* New York: Free Press.

———. 1979. *Before the best interests of the child.* New York: Free Press.

———. 1986. *In the best interests of the child.* New York: Free Press.

Landau, Hortense. 1974. Preparation and presentation for the juvenile court. In *National symposium in child abuse, 5th, Boston, 1974: Collected papers,* 74–78. Denver: American Humane Association, Children's Division.

Mayhall, Pamela D., and Katherine Eastlack Norgard. 1983. *Child abuse and neglect: Shared Responsibility.* New York: John Wiley and Sons. This is a generic overview of child maltreatment, which explores the range of issues related to defining, recognizing, and intervening in physical, sexual, and emotional maltreatment. It presents a particularly clear and organized layout of the formal response system and contains a solid review of the relevant literature in the field.

Miller, Baila, et al. 1982. System responses to initial reports of child abuse and neglect cases. *Journal of Social Service Research* 5 (3–4): 95–111.

Mnookin, Robert H. 1973. Foster care: In whose best interest? *Harvard Educational Review* 43 (4): 599–638. This renowned scholar illuminates the problems inherent in the "best interests of the child test" and considers its implications in the foster care decision-making process. Proposed criteria are presented and discussed in an in-depth and thought-provoking manner.

University of Chicago Law Review. 1968. Custody questions and child neglect, part 2. 35: 480.

Name Index

Subject Index

Abused child: characteristic behavior of, 57, 85–86, 90; destructive behavior of, 90–91; "high risk" children, 9; use of term, 5. *See also* Child maltreatment

Abusive parents: characteristics of, 6–9; feelings, ventilation of, 95–96; remembering in therapy, 46; resistance of, 24, 46; untreatable population, 41–42, 65

Acting-out children, residential treatment, 121

Activity groups, 83–85, 90–91; process, value of, 84

Adolescents, group approaches, 86–87; out-of-home placement, 113; terminating residential treatment, 125–27

AlAnon 171

Alcoholics Anonymous, 170

Alcoholism, definition of, 150; family life and, 156; incest and, 154; wet brain syndrome, 150. *See also* Substance abuse; Substance abusers.

American Association for Protecting Children, 6

Antabuse maintenance, 166–67

Apathy-futility syndrome, 8

Assessment, 25–29; for family therapy, 64–65; focus of, 26; for group therapy, 80–81; intake/investigative assessment, 25–26; interventive/continuous assessment, 25, 27; minority families, 132; nontraditional ap-

proach, necessity of, 29; of parental personality, 27; for residential treatment, 107; of social environment, 28–29; of substance abusers, 161–63

Authority: court-referred clients, 193; substance abusers, 163–64; use with parents, 48–49

Barriers to intervention, 32–34; conflicting societal values, 32–33; fragmentation of services, 31, 33; on institutional level, 33; pressures on worker, 33–34

Battered child, origin of term, 3, 4

Best interests test, 180

Black family, characteristics of, 129–30. *See also* Minority families

Blocking technique, family treatment, 76

Burnout, 34, 58; definition of, 58; factors in, 58–59

Case management, minority families, 145–46

Case manager, role of, 191

Central nervous system depressants, 151

Central nervous system stimulants, 152

Child Abuse Prevention and Treatment Act (1974), 4

Child characteristics, "high risk" children, 9

Child maltreatment: child factors, 9; definition of, 5; environmental factors, 10; frequency/scope of, 5; legal efforts